ANTIQUE SPANISH FURNITURE
MUEBLES ANTIGUOS ESPAÑOLES

ARMS OF CARLOS V (1500–1558), king of Spain and Holy Roman Emperor, persisted as a decorative motif on Spanish furniture for more than a century after his reign. This brass plaque, depicted here slightly smaller than actual size, is mounted on a velvet-covered XVII century chest in the collection of William E. Boggs, N. Y. Threadbare velvet in background is original.

ANTIQUE SPANISH FURNITURE

Muebles Antiguos Españoles

by

Rafael Doménech (Galissá)
&
Luis Pérez Bueno

Translated from the Spanish by
GRACE HARDENDORFF BURR

BILINGUAL EDITION
EDICION BILINGÜE

BONANZA BOOKS · NEW YORK

70-07731

LIBRARY OF CONGRESS CATALOG CARD NUMBER 64-25672

This edition published by Bonanza Books,
a division of Crown Publishers, Inc.,
by arrangement with The Archive Press, Inc.
a b c d e f g h

CONTENTS
TABLA DE MATERIAS

PLATES
LÁMINAS

PREFACE

Books on the history of Spanish furniture are rare in English. The long-neglected work of Rafael Doménech Gallisá and Luis Pérez Bueno —never translated into English and long out of print in Spanish—has become a classic reference work for the collector and the serious student. Despite the verbose, disorganized style of the introductory discourse on the art of furniture making (which has been edited vigorously in translation), the captions to the illustrations contain much practical information, and sharp insights into the aesthetics of furniture design.

The superb photographs—mostly of XVI- and XVII-century furniture—cover a broad selection of styles, and are large enough to permit detailed study of both structure and decoration. Similar pieces are grouped together to display the evolution of each type. Although the work devotes more space to furniture from palaces and mansions, there are several chests and tables, and a good number of chairs, in the so-called 'popular' style. Since there is no exact English equivalent of the Spanish word, 'popular', meaning 'of the people', I have sometimes used the word 'provincial' to denote these sturdy yet decorative little pieces, designed for everyday use in snug country rooms. The authors were fond of these specimens of 'popular' furniture because of their true Spanish identity, honest construction, and forceful ornament.

The authors of *Muebles,* Rafael Doménech Gallisá and Luis Pérez Bueno, were respectively Director and Curator of the old National Museum of Industrial Arts at Madrid. Created by Royal Decree in 1912, this institution was originally housed in humble surroundings on Sacramento Street in Madrid. Its purpose was to find, acquire, and preserve for exhibition, examples of the industrial arts of Spain, antique and modern, and Doménech was its first Direc-

tor. Thanks to his perseverance and drive, this purpose was achieved and indeed, expanded in scope. By the time of his death in 1929 his vision of a collection rivalling in quality, if not in quantity, the great decorative art museums of England and the Continent seemed within reach.

During these early years the authors collaborated to compile their book, and they published it in 1922. In 1930, after the death of Doménech, Pérez Bueno became Director of the Museum and in that year his little book, *El Mueble,* was published in the series *El tesoro artística de España;* it expanded the material in this volume and included illustrations covering a longer span of time. Pérez Bueno had previously written studies in the field of decorative arts, and later was to become especially known and honored for his study and works on Spanish glass. In 1943 he was received into the Academy of the Fine Arts of San Fernando, and elected to membership in the Hispanic Society of America. He died in 1954.

The professional careers of both men were devoted to enhancing the stature of the Museum and its collections. The facilities were greatly expanded in 1940 by removal to a renovated palace at 21 Montalbán Street, Madrid, and the name was changed to the National Museum of Decorative Arts. Its possessions now include magnificent collections of ceramics, glass, wood, leather and metal work, as well as tapestries and carpets. Its furniture collection contains more than 50 *vargueños,* 60 tables, 230 chairs, 80 chests and many other important pieces, and many of them are illustrated in this book.

In the United States, especially in Florida, California and the Southwest, a vigorous interest in Spanish furniture dates from the days of the Conquistadores; the spread of this interest to other areas testifies to the enduring appeal of Spanish cabinetwork.

In one of their extended captions Doménech and Pérez Bueno plead with designers for caution and restraint in the copying of the Museum's collection of carved motifs from old Spanish furniture for use on modern reproductions. Perhaps it is fortunate that they are not alive to see the application of grotesque parodies of Spanish motifs to the commercial furniture of our time: the use of pecan wood veneers, stained to imitate walnut planks; plastics disguised as leather; and cushions of urethane foam. Our simplified interiors dramatize the esthetic poverty of these reproductions and imitations, and confirm the authors' warning that sometimes decoration can destroy the beauty and even the purpose of a piece of furniture. Certainly the modern designer is hard pressed to match, on its own terms, the strength and harmony of straight lines, inlay, ironwork and carving that distinguishes the antique furniture of Spain.

I should like to acknowledge with gratitude the technical assistance of Mrs. Herbert Proske of New York, and of Mrs. Anton Klaus of Voorburg, Holland.

G.H.B.   December, 1964

INTRODUCCIÓN

I

No debe considerarse esta obra como un libro de historia del mueble español, ni aun como un ensayo de esa materia. Creemos que antes han de ponerse en circulación muchos documentos reales y escritos para que se pueda intentar esa historia. Todo el trabajo que al presente se hiciese en ese sentido sería prematuro, con todas las consecuencias que puedan dimanar de esta condición. Conformes con este criterio, en la presente obra sólo deseamos aportar documentos gráficos y directos de mobiliario español y algunas notas de documentos escritos. Tal vez en otro libro ampliemos estos materiales con gráficos tomados de antiguas obras de arte en que se reproducen muebles de la época.

La historia, como todo sistema de conocimientos humanos, está siempre en período de formación o de desarrollo.

Si nuevos conocimientos contribuyen a modificar y ampliar esos cuerpos sistemáticos del saber humano, también las orientaciones de la inteligencia, en cada época, determinan modificaciones y ampliaciones. Realmente no es esa una labor seminegativa de tejer y destejer, o derribar para construir de nuevo; es descubrir nuevas facetas o aspectos. La crítica histórica de una época que descubre aspectos nuevos en un orden de la actividad humana, podrá negar los aspectos antiguos y más si aquéllos revisten una gran novedad; pero esto no va más allá del orgullo de todo descubridor que no quiere aceptar una labor de colaboración o de aportación.

***

Debe tenderse a estudiar el arte del mueble (como todo arte), empleando la menor cantidad posible de hipótesis.

En todo trabajo histórico hay un gran margen de inferencia, siempre susceptible de ser rectificada; pero toda inferencia que no se base en gran documentación y sometida ésta a una labor crítica, será únicamente una exposición hipotética del pasado, que ninguna confianza debe merecer al lector.

Esas *construcciones* históricas, prematuras, misérrimas de elementos reales y escritos, frecuentemente suelen adornarse con una larga y brillante expresión literaria.

No hace mucho decíamos que, en todo libro de arte, el texto debe ilustrar a los gráficos y ese texto ha de ser muy sintético de conocimientos.

Una documentación gráfica, tan abundante como bien escogida, del mobiliario español o por lo menos radicado en España, permitirá a su vista agrupar tipos similares, determinar diferencias de estructura y de decoración y fijar modalidades en las evoluciones constructivas y artísticas de cada tipo. Esos trabajos sobre el mobiliario realizados en otros países, harán posible contrastar semejanzas, establecer diferencias y determinar influjos extranjeros en la ebanistería nacional. Porque los gráficos nos ofrecen toda la expresión técnica, en las múltiples variedades, que el principio de utilidad ha sido satisfecho en la vida de cada país y época y toda la impresión de sus sentimientos de belleza.

Respecto al mobiliario español, las fuentes de su conocimiento en sentido erudito, independiente de los muebles que hayan podido llegar hasta nosotros, son escasas. Los inventarios de los siglos medievales describen el mobiliario brevemente, fijándose más en la riqueza de la materia empleada que en los rasgos distintivos de su forma y caracteres de belleza decorativa. Consultando esos documentos sabremos, por ejemplo, de una arquilla, con todo detalle, la cantidad de oro y de plata que integraron su confección, y nada nos dirán respecto de los elementos decorativos que la embellecen, tales como sus esmaltes, repujados y cincelados.

En los ajuares—documentados—que se dieron a las princesas y damas principales, con motivo de sus bodas, ocurre igual. Se detallan las cosas para su avalúo, pero rara vez se detiene el foliculario (o quien ordenase la relación) en describir los caracteres artísticos del objeto inventariado.

Así van pasando, ante la vista del investigador, las arquillas, arcas o arcones, cofres o cofrecillos, según su dimensión; de maderas finas unos, tallados otros; encorados o forrados de terciopelo verde o carmesí; claveteados con clavazón dorada; y, del mismo modo, mesas, sillas, sillones, taburetes, escritorios, etc., etc.

En el mueble *cama*, es poco menos que imposible el hallar alguna nota que dé idea del material *madera* que entrara en su construcción; casi todas las descripciones anteriores al siglo XVI se concretan a la riqueza de los paños. En la lista de los regalos hechos a la Princesa Margarita de Austria cuando se casó con el príncipe D. Juan de Castilla el año 1497, de la única cama de que se habla es en los siguientes términos: «Una cama muy rica de tres paños de brocado carmesí de pelo y en medio de cada paño un escudo de las armas reales, las apañaduras dellos, chapadas de argentería de plata dorada o blanca, unas letras grandes con las divisas de los yugos que lleva el cielo de esta cama, cuatro goteras chapadas de la misma obra, forrado todo en lienzo bocarán...», etc., etc. En cambio, de unas pinturas sólo dice: «Unas tablas de nuestra Señora» y de una mesa: «Que está labrada toda de hueso con su banco de lo mismo.» En otros inventarios españoles de los siglos XIV y XV, se habla de arces grandes con dobles cerraduras, cofrecillos, arquillas de nogal labradas de ataracees, mesas entretalladas, guadamaciles con cenefas doradas, cielos de cama con medallones de guadamaciles, sillas de espaldar, braseros de plata, de hierro, con caja de palo (madera), cajas de latón labradas de ataujía y muebles «aparadores de madera con sus bancos». No dan los documentos escritos o impresos en esos tiempos mayor ilustración en esta materia. Han de pasar al-

gunos años, han de venir los escritores moralistas, poetas y dramaturgos de la segunda mitad del siglo XVI y todo el XVII para que, además de una prolija relación del mobiliario, nos presenten los muebles en el lugar y oficio que cada uno desempeñaba.

* * *

Del mueble de los primeros siglos de la Edad Media, lo mismo en España que en el extranjero, no hay núcleos para su estudio y comparación, existiendo sólo elementos aislados (ejemplares más o menos completos y simples fragmentos) donde lo serial, si existía, se ha perdido.

De esos ejemplares sueltos existen en España algunos, y de un gran valor arqueológico y con frecuencia también artístico.

De la tradición bizantina hay en la catedral de Gerona un sitial.

Un excelente medio de estudio del mobiliario de la alta Edad Media, nos lo dan las miniaturas de muchos códices: el *Vigiliano*, del Escorial; el de los *Testamentos*, de la catedral de Oviedo; de *San Beato*, de la Catedral de Gerona y de la Biblioteca Nacional de Madrid y el de los *Feudos*, en el Archivo de la Corona de Aragón.

Como monumentos reales de nuestro mobiliario en esa época, citaremos aquellos que pueden considerarse como más típicos y constitutivos, por lo tanto, de los ejemplares conductores del desarrollo técnico y artístico del mobiliario español, si bien con lagunas que tal vez puedan llenarse con el descubrimiento, hallazgo o conocimiento de otros ejemplares:

Sillas episcopales en piedra o mármol, como traducción de muebles que fueron construídos en madera u otro material.

La silla de tijera, que se supone perteneció a San Raimundo y se conserva en Roda (Aragón).

Los arcones y arcas de novia; el empleo de herrajes como elemento de utilidad (cierre y refuerzos) que llegó a convertirse en elemento decorativo, completándose con clavazón dorada y guadamaciles, según se lee en *El Poema del Cid*.

El cofrecillo relicario de San Millán de la Cogulla, en la Rioja, del tiempo de Sancho el Mayor; hállase en pésimo estado de conservación. El llamado *Cofre del Cid*, en Burgos; la serie de cofrecillos hispanoárabes de maravillosa labor (arqueta de la Cámara Santa, de Oviedo; las de Palencia, Astorga, Pamplona; la circular de la Seo de Zaragoza y la procedente de San Isidoro de León).

* * *

El estudio de la formación y desarrollo de la técnica del mueble constituye una de las enseñanzas más útiles que pueden sacarse de la historia, para el progreso de esa rama del arte decorativa.

El punto de partida en el mobiliario—como en todas las artes aplicadas—radica en la satisfacción de una necesidad de la vida humana. El mueble queda entonces reducido a un trabajo sencillo y tosco de carpintería. A medida que el mueble satisface la utilidad, comienza poco a poco el embellecimiento y nace entonces el arte del mueble y el ebanista como ejecutante.

La técnica constructiva es parecida en toda Europa: se ensambla o unen las piezas o tableros, a tope, a escuadra, con clavazón y el refuerzo en los ángulos, con enormes grapas de hierro (plancha más o menos gruesa y recortada) que alargando sus brazos por los tableros es ya un elemento decoravo, sin perder su valor utilitario de asegurar la resistencia del mueble. Cuando las uniones o ensamblajes se perfeccionan (de espiga, cola de golondrina...) disminuye el tamaño y la extensión de estas grapas, hasta casi llegar a desaparecer, como ocurre con el mobiliario de arcas y arquetas de poco volumen. Realmente este es el punto de partida de lo decorativo: convertir en elemento de belleza lo constructivo, sin desnaturalizar su función esencial de utilidad. Luego viene el depurar las formas de esos elementos constructivos en un alto sentido orgánico, esto es, adquiriendo la forma y proporciones debidas a la función de cada parte del mueble y a la relación de unas partes con otras (1) y por último acaba ese ciclo de lo decorativo, con el empleo de maderas ricas y otra clase de materiales suntuosos (bronce, plata, marfil, nácar, concha y hueso) y el empleo de una decoración superpuesta.

Abunda la madera en la Edad Media y el coste del aserrado es igual para el tablero grueso que el delgado, y así se emplean con preferencia los primeros (tableros de cinco y más centímetros de espesor, como puede verse en los arcones).

El arcón o arca es el mueble tipo que, en todos los países de Europa, desde la Edad Media puede servir como elemento de estudio y de comparación, por haber sido el mueble más usado y el de mayor utilidad: sirvió de asiento y de él nace el banco; sirvió de cama, etc.; y son hijuelas suyas y sus descendientes, arquillas, bufetillos, arquimesas y cuantas variedades de cajas ha habido en el mundo. Véanse tres etapas de desarrollo: 1.ª un solo cuerpo, como tal arcón; 2.ª dos cuerpos; la caja que se eleva para ser sostenida por un soporte, mesa o pie de arquerías; este pie, con cajonería llega a constituir la base del armario (2): 3.ª etapa o transición, cuando a esos dos cuerpos se les superpone un tercero. Luego, unificados los tres cuerpos habrán constituído el armario; un nuevo tipo de guardarropa. En el arcón puede estudiarse igualmente la técnica decorativa, aplicable, en general, a todo el mobiliario, ya que el arcón, decimos, es el mueble capital en esos tiempos. Se tallan los frentes; el espesor de los tableros permite hacerlo con facilidad, principalmente en el nogal; también se pintan, se policroman y estofan con la preparación y procedimientos de las obras de pintura en los retablos de la época. Reminiscencias de esa pintura sobre los muebles perduran en temas geométricos y diminuta flora, con carácter de labores españolas, inconfundibles con las italianas a fines del siglo XV y durante el XVI; principalmente en la cajonería de nuestras arquilas, de tipo más popular que suntuoso.

Esa decoración pintada substituía, con economía en la mano de obra, a la que por entonces se hacía incrustando — labor de taracea — con marfil o hueso y trozos de maderas teñidas. Debe citarse como un magnífico ejemplo de arcón pintado, el que guarda los restos de San Isidro, en Madrid.

(1) Creemos que ningún ejemplo puede ser más educativo que el desarrollo constructivo del orden dórico griego.

(2) Y el origen de la cómoda, mueble que los artistas franceses, en los llamados estilos de los Luises, tanto embellecieron sin perder aquella condición de práctica utilidad, de reconocida *comodidad*, base del gran desarrollo y uso que tuvo en Europa.

Los elementos característicos del arte gótico trascienden, con el natural retraso desde la piedra (lo monumental) al mueble, y las superficies de tableros (de arcones, respaldos de sitiales, etc.) se tallan con la agilidad y primor que requería la belleza de las arquerías, las sutilísimas columnillas, florones, cresterías, etc. y cuando llega el periodo florido, se facilita el trabajo y permite que sea menor el espesor de los tableros, el superponer sobre estos, encoladas, las tallas góticas, como un encaje de madera. Igual sistema o proceso se siguió en las tablas y retablos religiosos al encuadrarlos o enmarcarlos con tallas sobrepuestas.

Hemos de ampliar los datos antes consignados sobre las arcas. En el siglo XV van cubiertas o vestidas con un tejido (ensayaladas); están los cofres *encorados*, esto es, forrados de cuero labrado, liso, tachonado, etc. El *arcaz* es una gran arca con dos o más cerraduras.

Las arquetas se trabajan en nogal, labradas con *atarcèes*, recubiertas con chapas de metal (plata o latón) relevadas y cinceladas, y también esmaltadas o con cuero labrado y hermosos herrajes.

Al ocuparnos de esos muebles debemos hacer constar que, en los escritos antiguos, indistintamente se llaman arquimesa, arquilla, caja papelera y mueble escritorio. La palabra *bufete* se aplica más a mueble de comedor y es francesa; pero en algunos escritores clásicos castellanos se lee *bufetillo*, para designar (al parecer) un mueble escritorio de secreto para joyas, etc.

Del período gótico la documentación real es muy abundante y se completa, tanto en los detalles (muebles sueltos) como en los conjuntos (su disposición según las habitaciones y clases sociales), en libros miniados—el *Libro de las Cántigas*, del Escorial, y otros—en las obras pictóricas de tablas y muros y en los sellos reales.

Entre el número abundante de muebles góticos que se conservan deben mencionarse las sillerías de coro, si bien, tanto éstas como los grandes armarios de las sacristías, por su colocación fija, deben ser tratados aparte. Asimismo, por las relaciones artísticas y técnicas con el mueble, los artesonados y puertas ofrecen un interés muy grande cuando se trata del estudio del mobiliario,

pudiendo incluirse en él dentro de un amplio concepto de esa materia.

Huelga citar las magníficas sillerías de coro góticas y del Renacimiento que poseen las catedrales españolas, unas trabajadas por artistas extranjeros, otras por artífices españoles.

Como sitiales o sillas reales debe mencionarse la del Rey D. Martín, en la catedral de Barcelona, ejecutada en plata dorada, pero bajo el influjo de los trabajos de madera; entre las sillas episcopales, quizá la más notable es la silla del oficiante en la Cartuja de Miraflores, de Burgos.

Poseemos un gran número de artesonados mudéjares de un valor técnico y artístico grandísimo. Respecto a otros trabajos mudéjares en madera que directamente se refieren al arte del mueble, sólo conocemos los siguientes: el Tríptico relicario del Monasterio de Piedra (hoy en la Real Academia de la Historia) construído en 1390 y que tiene la disposición de un armario; la célebre alacena llamada de los Templarios que existe en Londres en el Museo Victoria and Albert y procede de Toledo; la sobrepuerta de Santa Fe en la ciudad imperial y el pequeño órgano de la Catedral vieja de Salamanca.

* * *

Hay una técnica decorativa del mueble que adquiere gran desarrollo en Italia, a partir del siglo XV y se extiende por Europa durante el Renacimiento; nos referimos a la *tarsia, delicioso poema pictórico* que ha dicho un artista italiano, que si en los comienzos del siglo XIV apunta tímidamente sus labores geométricas, en los comienzos del XVI llega a la cumbre de su gloria.

En rigor de verdad, su origen es oriental y procede del arte del mosaico; decorar un mueble con la incrustación de maderas de diversos colores, marfil, hueso y más adelante chapas de latón recortadas formando dibujos. Esa técnica ha recorrido modalidades artísticas tan variadas como las *taraceas* árabes españolas y los decorados imitando verdaderos cuadros, de los italianos.

En España el tipo de taraceas de elementos poligonales comenzó a cultivarse, tal vez, en el Califato de Córdoba; arraigó en Murcia, en Málaga y principalmente en Granada, donde perduró el tipo tradicional, en sillones y cajas, casi hasta nuestros días, pudiéndose denominar a esos trabajos labores andaluzas, por estar en España casi circunscrita su fabricación en la zona andaluza.

En Cataluña la taracea de madera de haya sobre nogal dió lugar a un tipo muy característico en los llamados *cofres de obra de Gerona;* otro tipo catalán es el de la taracea de hueso sobre nogal, en una decoración hecha con pequeñas labores y de un marcado carácter oriental; se le llama *pinyonet* y ese trabajo ha continuado casi hasta nuestros días, como la taracea andaluza.

* * *

La arquitectura del Renacimiento, con sus formas constructivas y sus temas y composiciones decorativas, influye directamente sobre el mueble, como ocurrió en la época gótica. En el siglo XVI se extiende el nuevo estilo por Europa y llega a España. Se construye el mobiliario de frentes arquitectónicas, como si fueran pequeños modelos, ejecutados en madera y bronces, de las portadas de los templos católicos; han cambiado las formas, pero no el concepto de los siglos anteriores.

Toman en cada país una estructura genérica con modalidad propia, siendo la española sobria y serena de líneas, cuya síntesis se halla en Herrera.

En España durante el siglo XVI se construye el mobiliario civil y el religioso (que por su aplicación especial tiene características muy diferenciales del otro, en la mayoría de los casos) tan lujoso y rico, por sus materiales y decoración, como el mejor que por esa época se hiciera en Francia, Alemania e Inglaterra. Solamente las obras italianas podían competir y aún superar, dentro de su peculiar estilo, con nuestros armarios, arquillas, cofres, bufetillos, marcos, relicarios, etcétera, incrustados de marfiles, nácares y concha, con ricas aplicaciones de plata labrada y bronces dorados a fuego.

Nuestro mobiliario del siglo XVI y gran parte del XVII, salvo inevitables influencias en las copias y reproducciones que se hicieron de muebles belgas, holandeses y franceses, es perfecto en su técnica constructiva y decorativa. Tenía que ser así, por ser sus obras producto de los pequeños talleres nacidos al amparo de la enseñanza que,

en las artes de la madera, habían dado los grandes escultores del Renacimiento que acudieron a Barcelona, Salamanca, Valladolid y Toledo, principalmente, para esculpir y ensamblar en los templos, maravillosos retablos, sillerías de coro, púlpitos y facistoles.

Ofrece gran interés el estudio del mobiliario de un país—creación, desarrollo, transformaciones, etc.—Con rarísimas excepciones, del examen de los muebles españoles de los siglos XVI y XVII, podríamos deducir que en la infinita variedad de armarios, arcas, cajas, mesas, sillas, sillones, etcétera, reina el anónimo. En la mayoría de los casos no sabemos del lugar en que se fabricaron (1) y quienes fueron sus artífices, porque los maestros que les dieron vida, encerrados en humilde modestia, rara vez pusieron su firma o monograma en esas obras. Realmente en el mobiliario civil, hasta fines del siglo XVII y durante el XVIII, en toda Europa son raros los casos en que pueda determinarse la paternidad de alguna obra hasta que se destacan ebanistas insignes en Italia y principalmente en Inglaterra y Francia, bien por ser creadores o hábiles transformadores de formas y decorados, o por contar con la resuelta protección de los monarcas que les encargaban el mobiliario de sus palacios, dándose con ello ejemplo y normas que seguían los nobles y la burguesía más acomodada.

Perdemos en España nuestras características en el mueble nacional a medida que avanza el siglo XVII y en el XVIII por completo, desde que la dinastía Borbónica ocupa su trono y lógicamente predominan los estilos llamados de los Luises, en muchos casos llenos de elegancia y movimiento de líneas, tan en oposición, por sus curvas y ligerezas, con la robustez y simplicidad de los nuestros.

Por eso, la investigación y estudio de lo que pudo ser el mobiliario español en las pasadas centurias, ha de hacerse y casi limitarse hasta los comienzos del siglo XVIII. Pero, bien entendido,

(1) De los famosos *Vargueños* que según la tradición se *crearon* en Vargas pueblo de la provincia de Toledo, nada de cierto se sabe; sólo sí que, en Vargas, ni en tradición se conserva recuerdo de que allí hubiese habido jamás carpintería o taller de esos muebles, ni de ningunos otros.—Posible es que el nombre de Vargueño les venga de un taller que hubo en Toledo, en el siglo XVI, cuyo dueño, maestro entallador y ebanista (diríamos ahora), se llamaba Vargas. Esa opinión la hemos oído sustentar al ceramista de Toledo, don Sebastián Aguado, por datos antiguos que ha llegado a conocer.

este es nuestro pensar, que aunque los ebanistas españoles hicieran muebles en el siglo XVIII y parte del XIX siguiendo la moda de los *patrones* extranjeros, jamás acertaron a expresar con pureza esos estilos.

Siempre a través de esas copias y formas debidas a extrañas inspiraciones, se observa en las obras españolas una síntesis de fortaleza algo ruda y la falta de flexibilidad en la expresión de la línea, muy en armonía con el carácter nuestro. Después de todo, más vale así; porque acusa en este aspecto una constante permanencia de la personalidad, en el correr de los siglos.

Dentro de la influencia italiana que se dejó sentir en España durante el Renacimiento, siguieron, sin embargo, predominando los arcones cuadrangulares y planos en la cubierta.

El arcón y el cofre mueren cuando aparece la cómoda, y al armario se da una gran importancia en el ajuar de las habitaciones. El arcón y cofre eran aún de uso corriente en el siglo XVII.

* * *

La historiografía del mueble español, a partir del Renacimiento, es posible con la cantidad de ejemplares reales hoy conocidos y con la rica documentación escrita que poseemos.

En los siglos XV y XVI se citan los «aparadores de madera con sus *vancos*». Estos aparadores eran (según puede interpretarse de la lectura de los inventarios) guardarropas o armarios para guardarlas.

Muchas veces a la mesa se la denomina y describe «una tabla con sus *vancos*»; fueron ésas, grandes mesas donde debían comer las gentes del servicio de las casas principales.

Los novelistas del siglo XVII citan —entre muchos muebles— escritorios de ébano y marfil; braseros de plata con cajas de ébano y marfil. Navarrete en su obra *Restauración política de España*, habla del excesivo lujo que había en el mobiliario de las casas en tiempos de Felipe III y cita escritorios y tantos y tan varios bufetes, unos embutidos en diversas piedras, otros de plata, otros de ébano y marfil y otras mil diferencias de maderas traídas de Asia.

Ese desarrollo del lujo originó ciertas disposiciones Reales. Para los muebles y metales preciosos que en ellos se podían emplear, Felipe II dió en Aranjuez una, en 15 de Mayo de 1593, para evitar que los vendedores engañasen a los compradores en el peso de la plata, prohibiendo a plateros y doradores que hiciesen, vendieran y compraran escritorios, arquillas, braseros, chapivés, mesas, contadores, etc., ni ningún otro objeto de plata batida, relevada, etc. Creemos que esta disposición fué consecuencia de lo pedido por los procuradores en las cortes de Madrid (1563) en las que dijeron que se consumía para dorar y platear el hierro, la madera y los metales, en estos reinos, mucho oro y plata del que nadie podía servirse, perdiéndose, y entonces pedían que, a no ser para el culto divino y para las armas y aparejos para la gineta y aderezos de la brida, que no se dorase o plateara el hierro, madera, cobre ni metal alguno. Contestó el monarca que consultaría a su consejo y proveería lo que conviniera. Esas disposiciones no sólo afectaron a los muebles propiamente dichos, sino al complemento del mobiliario en la casa, durante los siglos XVI y XVII, como fueron cortinajes, cielos y colgaduras de camas, doseles y tapicerías para los muros.

Esas leyes prohibitivas se dieron principalmente desde el reinado de Felipe II hasta el de Carlos II; casi siempre fueron ineficaces.

* * *

Son una excelente fuente histórica los estudios que se han hecho sobre las asociaciones gremiales en España.

En Cataluña esos estudios arrancan desde Capmany y en Valencia, de Tramoyeres Blasco. En Castilla (sobre todo en Madrid), el gremio de entalladores y ensambladores se gobernaba por ordenanzas aprobadas por los años de 1588. A este gremio se unió luego el de ebanistas, formando, desde fines del siglo XVII, un mismo cuerpo gremial.

* * *

Los más graves escritores del tiempo de Felipe III clamaron contra la afición a lo extranjero. En todas las artes hemos sufrido esa influencia y ha tenido el público esas aficiones, con sobrada frecuencia. Hoy se repiten las diatribas contra lo extranjero y se habla y también se trata de crear un arte español, así por programas y con un cultivo de caldo cerebral.

Ahora como antaño, la intención, el propósito no pueden ser mejores; envuelven un íntimo sentir de amor patrio. Es un noble orgullo creado y sostenido a través de nuestras grandezas pretéritas que se exacerba viendo nuestras artes industriales menospreciadas y hundidas en el olvido, con cuenta y razón de las extrañas que, principalmente desde los comienzos del siglo XVIII, invadieron nuestros mercados abastando casi por sí solas todas las necesidades nacionales.

La realidad del arte, que es una de las realidades más importantes de la vida, no se crea ni, por tanto, puede llegar a fomentarse con manifestaciones de dolor, de amargura ni de protesta iracunda. La realidad exige creación, y la creación no se rinde en la vida con sólo el artificio de la palabra por elocuente y sincera que sea.

Fundamentalmente, fatalmente podremos decir, fué viniendo lo extranjero cuando lo nacional dejó de producirse en la cuantía necesaria o se produjo con inferioridad.

Cierto es que podemos tener un gran orgullo y sentirnos muy españoles al contemplar las mejores obras de la verdadera pintura contemporánea, porque han tenido grandes precedentes en los tres artistas más geniales de España. Greco, Velázquez y Goya. Pero nosotros no podemos sentir orgullo ante la cerámica de Alcora, porque artística y aun técnicamente, se produjo imitando lo extranjero... porque nosotros no sabíamos hacerla tan bien como los extranjeros en el siglo XVIII. El problema consiste en no llegar a una manifiesta inferioridad frente a la producción de otros países. Debe tenderse, pues, a promover de un modo racional y no artificioso, el progreso de nuestras industrias artísticas. La del mueble técnicamente se produce en España tan bien como en otro país; artísticamente nos hallamos en un grado no pequeño de inferioridad. No basta con tender a una perfección del arte del mobiliario (como de otro cualquiera); la victoria no se obtendrá atendiendo sólo al perfeccionamiento de

una industria artística, sino a la totalidad (1). El arte del mueble depende estrechamente de la vida de las otras artes; el sostenimiento vigoroso de un estilo es lo fundamental, pues ese estilo es el que da personalidad a todo arte aplicado.

Cuando ese estilo no existe en una nación, sus artes industriales han de vivir a expensas del estilo o de los estilos más preeminentes en el extranjero.

Crear un estilo nacional, ya decíamos antes que no es obra que se haga sólo por la voluntad y con esfuerzos de inteligencia. La primera condición, la que es esencial en toda actividad artística, es poseer una gran sensibilidad estética; muchas gentes se engañan creyendo tenerla porque se admiran contemplando las obras antiguas que alaban los libros, o de las contemporáneas que enaltecen personas cultas. Esa sensibilidad no se forma con poca o mucha erudición del pasado. Todo el mundo puede aprender las características externas de un estilo; sólo los que tienen temperamento apto podrán *sentir* las bellezas de un estilo. Pero hay muchas gentes a las que se les pervierte ese sentido de lo estético, por usarlo erróneamente, o se les atrofia por falta de aplicación.

Otra condición esencial es la de mirar el arte de frente y no de reojo o volviendo la cabeza hacia atrás. Se ha dicho con gran acierto de la verdad que, en las artes, el punto de partida es el natural, pero no el de llegada. En todas las artes y muy especialmente en las decorativas, se puede decir que el punto de partida es el pasado, pero en modo alguno puede ser el de llegada. Detenerse en lo histórico es matar el porvenir del arte, porque el porvenir es opuesto al pasado, y el porvenir es la vida y el pasado es historia, arqueología, labor contemplativa y no creadora.

Una tercera condición que afecta a la esencia de las artes decorativas, es la lógica. El punto de partida de esa lógica está en la utilidad que debe cumplir todo edificio o todo objeto de arte decorativo. El principio de lo útil es el germen de toda modernidad y de toda originalidad en esas artes; nace de la vida que se realiza y esa vida, cuanto

---

(1) Porque ninguna se produce aisladamente, independientemente.

más potente es, es más moderna y más nacional, pero también más se desplaza fuera de sus fronteras.

Ese principio de lo útil determina clara e imperiosamente la estructura, por ejemplo, de un mueble, y de esa determinación nace su forma. Esa estructura se perfecciona y la forma se hace más depurada y bella; con sólo esos caracteres se llega a un trabajo original, a un arte con personalidad propia. Viene luego lo decorativo; las simples formas constructivas se visten con formas naturales, geométricas o libres, para conseguir un máximo de belleza; *jamás esas formas mejorarán las constructivas, pero es fácil que alguna vez destruyan su belleza y aun parte de su utilidad;* todos conocemos muebles poco útiles o incómodos, *por culpa del arte. Del arte mal entendido y peor aplicado.*

El estudio detenido de un buen número de ejemplos de muebles antiguos, puede enseñar mucho en esas cuestiones fundamentales del arte del mobiliario, encaminadas a su producción y no sólo a una simple e infecunda actividad contemplativa.

* * *

Lo popular tiene en el arte español un valor de primer orden, no superado por el de los países de la Antigua Rusia y centro de Europa. Un estudio de esa modalidad del arte no puede realizarse en breve espacio, y tal vez en plazo no largo podamos ofrecerla al público.

En el presente volumen se dan un buen número de ejemplos de nuestro mobiliario popular, tanto porque sus rasgos bien enérgicos pueden servir para mostrar los caracteres eminentes de ese arte en España, cuanto por ser las formas de esos muebles fuente de un trabajo bien original. Siempre y cuando se sepan hallar esos elementos generadores y haya temperamento artístico para su desarrollo.

El arte popular ha venido gozando en España de un gran predicamento en estos últimos años y los únicos resultados prácticos que se han conseguido han sido recoger y evitar la destrucción de un buen número de ejemplares de muebles, bordados, cerámica, etc. Tal vez una de las colecciones más completas la posee el Museo Nacional de Artes Industriales, de Madrid.

Se ha pretendido que los motivos populares en la decoración, como en música, podían substituir a una verdadera inspiración artística y en esto se ha sufrido un gran engaño. El motivo popular, en arte decorativo, es más difícil emplearlo de un modo original que un tema sacado de las formas naturales. La simple copia no ha podido dar más que resultados negativos para un arte nuevo y para el popular que ha quedado desnaturalizado.

Se ha pretendido también ornar la casa ciudadana con ejemplares de ese arte popular. El trasplante ha sido ridículo.

INTRODUCTION

ANTIQUE SPANISH FURNITURE

This book is not a history of Spanish furniture, nor even an essay about it. Many documents have to be unearthed before such a book can be written; anything else would be premature. We have merely presented a collection of Spanish pieces with a few comments based on our research.

History, like any field of human knowledge, is always changing. New discoveries change and add to human knowledge, and critical judgment modifies it. In a century that seeks new outlooks and methods, historical criticism may contradict earlier viewpoints, particularly if the new views are radically different; this tendency reflects only the pride of the discoverer who refuses to admit any assistance.

One should study the art of furniture (like all art) by avoiding hypothesis as much as possible. In all historical work, inferences are subject to confirmation or correction, but any inference not founded on a critical study of documents would be of no value to the reader. In books on art the text should explain the illustrations by supplying facts, not theories.

An illustrated book with many well chosen examples of furniture permits grouping similar types together to show the differences of structure and decoration, and the evolution of each type. By studying foreign publications the serious student can compare similarities, establish differences, and determine foreign influences on Spanish cabinetwork.

Sources of information about Spanish furniture, aside from the surviving pieces themselves, are scarce. Inventories from medieval centuries describe furniture very briefly, concentrating more on the richness of the material than on form and decorative beauty. One such document refers, for example, to a small metal chest; the amount of gold and silver in its composition is given in minute detail, but nothing is said about how it was decorated—whether with enameling, *repoussé,* or chasing.

Similarly, in accounts of the trousseaus given to princesses and noblewomen possessions are enumerated for their value, and the writer seldom bothers with artistic details. Small chests, large chests (*arcones*), coffers or coffrets are listed according to size: some of fine woods, some carved; others covered with leather or green or crimson velvet, fastened with gilded nails. Tables, chairs, armchairs, stools, secretaries, and other pieces are listed in the same way.

As for beds, it is almost impossible to learn what kind of wood was used in their construction; almost all descriptions before the XVI century concentrate on the richness of the hangings. The list of gifts presented to Princess Margaret of Austria when she married Prince Don Juan of Castile in 1497 describes "A very rich bed with three lengths of crimson pile brocade, and in the middle of each piece a shield with the royal arms, their trimmings enriched with *appliqué* of silver or silver gilt. Some large letters with the emblem of the yoke are on the canopy. There are four valances trimmed with *appliqué* in the same way, all lined with buckram," and so on. Conversely, some paintings are listed only as "Some pictures of our Lady," and a table and bench as "all inlaid with bone." Other Spanish inventories of the XIV and XV centuries mention great chests with double locks, small walnut chests inlaid with marquetry, tables carved in bas-relief, embossed leather wall-hangings (*guademeciles*) with gilded borders, bed canopies with embossed leather medallions, chairs with backs, silver and iron braziers with wooden stands, boxes of damascened brass, and wooden buffets with benches. Other written or printed documents of the period give no better description. Eventually the writers, poets and dramatists of the second half of the XVI century began to describe the placement of furniture and how it was used.

In Spain as elsewhere, there is no nucleus for the study and comparison of the furniture of the early Middle Ages, since the badly damaged examples and fragments that survive provide no continuity of development. Some of the surviving pieces in Spain have great archaeological and artistic value, such as a bishop's throne in the Cathedral of Gerona, which dates to the Romanesque period.

The furniture of the late Middle Ages can be studied more easily, particularly from the miniatures in many old manuscripts including the *Vigiliano* and the *Libro de las Cántigas* in the *Escorial;* the *Testaments,* in Oviedo Cathedral; *San Beato,* in the Cathedral of Gerona and the *Biblioteca Nacional* at Madrid; and the *Feudos,* in the archives of the Crown of Aragón.

As monuments of our furniture at that time, we have selected the most typical examples, which show the technical and artistic development of Spanish furniture. Of course there remain gaps that must be filled by the discovery of information about other examples: bishops' thrones in stone or marble, copied from pieces of furniture which were made of wood or another material; or the X-shaped chair that is supposed to have belonged to *San Raimundo* and is preserved at Roda (Aragón); large trunks and hope chests; functional ironwork (locks and hinges) that gradually evolved into decorative elements, supplemented by gilded nails and embossed leather (according to *El Poema del Cid*); the small reliquary of *San Millán de la Cogulla,* in La Rioja of the time of *Sancho el Mayor;* the so-called *Cofre del Cid* at Burgos; and the series of small Hispano-Moresque coffrets of marvelous workmanship, including the chest of the *Cámara Santa,* Oviedo; those at Palencia, Astorga, and Pamplona; the cylindrical box of the *Seo* at Zaragoza and the one from *San Isidoro,* León.

Furniture, like all applied art, evolved from the desire to satisfy a necessity of human life. In the Middle Ages it was only a simple, crude piece of carpentry. Little by little, embellishment began; furniture-making became an art, and the cabinetmaker appeared.

The techniques of construction were the same all over Europe: wood was abundant, and since thick or thin planks cost the same, cabinetmakers used thick ones. Boards used in the construction of chests were often two or more inches thick. They were joined or united end to end at right angles, with nails and bracing angles, and enormous cramp irons (of varying thickness) that both braced and decorated the wooden-plank furniture. After the development of the mortise and tenon joint, the size and length of the cramp diminished until it almost disappeared—as it did, in fact, in little coffers.

Decoration evolves from an attempt to change structural elements into things of beauty without doing away with their essential function. As the structural elements change and become proportioned according to the function of each part of furniture and its relation to the others, the form becomes purified until the decorative cycle finally ends with the use of applied decoration, rich woods, bronze, silver, ivory, mother-of-pearl, shell and bone.

The trunk or chest can be used to compare and study the furniture of all the countries of Europe from the time of the Middle Ages, because it was the commonest and most useful piece of furniture. It often served as a seat and as a bed, and its offspring and descendants include not only little chests, sideboards, writing desks, and boxes, but also the bench. This development took place in three stages. First, a single unit such as the chest. Second, two parts, with the chest raised on a support like a table or a trestle stand, the stand with drawers evolving into the base of a clothes press.[1] Third, a stage or transition when these two parts supported a third. When the three parts were combined, they comprised the clothes press, a new type of wardrobe.

Similarly, by studying chests one can trace the decorative techniques employed on all furniture. The fronts, made of walnut, were easy to carve because of their thickness. Gothic carving was born in stone and spread slowly to furniture.

The wooden surfaces of chests, the backs of chairs of honor, and similar pieces were carved with lightness and dexterity in beautiful arcades, in slender colonnettes, rosettes and cresting. When the ornate period arrived, cabinetmakers used thinner wood and their work became easier because instead of carving the plank itself, they glued small carvings to its surface, giving a lacy effect. The same system of superimposing decorations on wood was used on the framework of panels and altarpieces.

Sometimes they were also painted in polychrome or gilt, like the altar pieces of the time. Surviving traces of painting on our furniture depict geometric designs and small flowers; these were characteristic of Spanish craftsmen (and should not be confused with Italian designs) from the end of the XV through the XVI century. They occur especially on the drawers of little chests, and are executed in a style more popular than elegant. Painted decoration was an economical substitute for inlay done with ivory, bone, or pieces of stained wood. A magnificent example is the painted chest that holds the remains of *San Isidro* in Madrid.

In the XV century some chests were covered with fabric, or leather bound—that is, covered with tooled, plain, or embossed leather, particularly the *arcaz,* a massive chest with two or more locks. Small chests were made of walnut, often inlaid, or covered with plates of embossed and chased silver or brass; some were enameled or covered with tooled leather and beautiful iron-work.

In medieval writings, no distinction is made between *arquimesa, arquilla, caja papelera,* and *mueble escritorio.* All these words were used to mean writing desk. The French word *bufete* is more applicable to a piece of dining-room furniture, but in some of the classic Castilian authors one reads the word *bufetillo* (small desk) used apparently to designate a writing desk with hiding places for jewels and other valuables.

A relatively large number of documents relating to furniture survives from the Gothic period. Individual pieces of furniture as well as the general arrangement in different kinds of houses and for different social classes are represented in illuminated manuscripts, mural or panel paintings and on royal seals.

Choir stalls are among the abundant Gothic furniture that survives, even though they, like the large clothes presses in sacristies, because of their fixed position, really fall in the province of architecture, as do the panelled ceilings and doors of churches. Nevertheless, because of artistic and technical similarities they are of great interest to the student of furniture, and might be included in a wider study. It is needless to cite the magnificent Gothic and Renaissance choir-stalls in Spanish cathedrals, although some were made by foreign artists.

Among the surviving Gothic seats of honor or throne chairs is the one of King Martin in Barcelona Cathedral, made of silver gilt, with the design influenced by carvings in wood. Perhaps the most notable throne is that of the presiding bishop in the Carthusian Monastary of Miraflores near Burgos.

Spain still possesses many *mudéjar* ceilings of great technical and artistic value, but relatively few *mudéjar* works in wood that are directly related to the art of furniture. We can cite only the reliquary tryptych of the *Monasterio de Piedra* (now in the *Real Academia de la Historia*), built in 1390, which has the appearance of a wardrobe; the famous "cupboard of the Templars" from Toledo, now in the Victoria and Albert Museum in London; the overdoor of *Santa Fe* in the Imperial City; and the small organ from the old Cathedral of Salamanca.

One technique for the decoration of furniture developed rapidly in Italy at the end of the XV century and spread through Europe during the Renaissance. This was intarsia, a "lovely pictorial poem" as an Italian artist has said. Although at the beginning of the XIV century this style used geometric designs timidly, by the beginning of the XVI century, when intarsia reached its apex, geometric designs predominated.

Strictly speaking, this technique is oriental in origin and springs from mosaic art: that is, decorating furniture with inlay of different coloured woods, ivory, bone, and later pierced brass plates forming pictures. In Spain this technique has gone through a variety of artistic styles, from Hispano-Moresque geometrical inlay and decorations to the making of real pictures that imitated those of the Italians.

In our furniture, the geometrical inlay of polygonal pieces began perhaps in the Caliphate of Córdoba. It took root in Murcia, in Málaga, and chiefly in Granada, where the traditional form has lasted almost to this day on chairs and chests. These works are now called 'Andalusian' because in Spain manufacture was limited almost entirely to that region. In Cataluña the inlay of beech wood over walnut gave rise to a very characteristic type on the so-called chests of Gerona (*cofres de obra Gerona*). Another Catalan type involves the inlay of bone on walnut, forming a decoration made of tiny pieces with a strong oriental flavor; it is called *pinyonet,* and like the Andalusian technique, continues to the present day.

Renaissance architecture, with its structural forms, themes, decorations and compositions, directly influenced furniture just as Gothic architecture had done. In the XVI century the new style spread through Europe and reached Spain. Furniture was constructed with architectural facades in wood and bronze that looked like small models of church doors. Forms changed, but not the concepts and ideas of preceding centuries.

Each country expresses its own characteristics in a particular form of structure, Spain's being sobriety and serenity of line, whose synthesis is found in the work of Herrera, architect to Philip II, builder of the Escorial. During the XVI century Spanish secular and religious furniture was built with such luxurious and rich materials and decoration that it equaled the best of France, Germany, and England. Italian pieces were the only ones that could compete with and even surpass our cabinets, chests, coffers, small buffets, frames, and reliquaries adorned with ivory, mother-of-pearl and shell, with rich applications of chased silver and gilded bronze.

Our furniture of the XVI century and a great part of the XVII, except for some inevitable influences from Belgian, Dutch and French pieces, is superb in construction and decoration. This was natural, because the furniture was a product of small workshops fostered by the great sculptors of the Renaissance, who taught the art of carving wood. They gathered in Barcelona, Salamanca, Valladolid and Toledo to carve and assemble extraordinary altar pieces, choir-stalls, pulpits and lecterns.

And yet, with very rare exceptions, the makers of the Spanish furniture of the XVII and XVIII centuries chose to remain anonymous. In most cases we know neither the place where the furniture was made nor the craftsmen who made it because the cabinetmakers were too humble or modest to put their mark or initials on their work.[2] In secular furniture, before the end of the XVII and the XVIII century the authorship of a particular piece can rarely be determined. This changed with the rise of famous cabinetmakers in Italy, England and France, noted either for being creators—or able adapters—of form and decoration, or because kings who were their patrons put them in charge of the palace furniture, thereby setting an example which the nobility and more wealthy bourgeois followed.

Spain gradually lost her national traits in furniture toward the end of the XVII century. In the XVIII they completely disappeared during the rule of the Bourbons, when the dominant styles were naturally those called "Louis", which in many cases were full of elegance and restlessness of line, whose curves and graces sharply conflicted with Spain's characteristic robustness and simplicity.

We feel that the investigation and study of antique Spanish furniture should end at the beginning of the XVIII century. Although Spanish cabinetmakers produced furniture in the XVIII and part of the XIX centuries following foreign fashions in design, they never succeeded in expressing these styles in a pure form. When made by Spanish craftsmen these copies and imitations always give an impression of rude strength and rigidity of line very much in harmony with the Spanish character. After all, one still can note a constancy of personality which runs through all the ages.

With the examples and rich documentation available, it is possible to trace clearly the historiography of furniture from the end of the Renaissance. In the XV and XVI centuries "cupboards of wood with their stands" are recorded. According to what we can derive from reading the inventories these cupboards were wardrobes or clothes closets.

Under the Italian influence, which was felt in Spain during the Renaissance, quadrangular chests with flat tops prevailed. The chest and coffer remained popular during the XVII century, but vanished when the bureau appeared, and the wardrobe gained great importance in household furnishings. Tables were often described as planks with trestles; these were huge tables where the servants of important families ate.

Novelists of the XVII century cite, among many pieces of furniture, desks of ebony and ivory, and silver braziers with ebony and ivory stands. Navarrete in his work *Restauración política de España* talks about the excessive luxury of the household furnishings during the reign of Philip III, and as examples he describes writing desks and buffets, some inlaid with different stones, some made of silver, and others of ebony and ivory and a thousand exotic woods from Asia.

This display of luxury persisted despite several royal decrees regarding furniture and the precious metals that could be used on it. In 1593 Philip II gave an order to prevent sellers from deceiving customers about the weight of silver, and to prohibit silversmiths and gilders from making, selling and buying desks, chests, braziers, *chapivés,* tables, or any object of beaten or embossed silver. This order was probably the result of a demand by attorneys in the courts of Madrid (1563), who argued that it was wasteful to gild and silverplate wood, iron, and other metals, since this removed too much gold and silver from circulation. They asked that gold and silver not be used except for religious objects, arms, and horse furniture. During the XVI and XVII centuries, these prohibitive laws affected not only furniture but also curtains, canopies, bed hangings and tapestries.

The records of trade guilds, and the laws regulating them, comprise another excellent historical source for information about XVII century furniture. In Cataluña these studies started with Capmany and in Valencia with Tramoyores

Blasco. In Castile (above all in Madrid) the guild of wood carvers and joiners was governed by ordinances passed about the year 1588. Cabinetmakers joined this guild, forming one body, towards the end of the XVII century.

The most serious writers of the time of Philip III spoke out against foreign influences. In all the arts Spain has been open to these influences, and all too often public taste supported them. Today foreign taste is denounced in an attempt to preserve a truly Spanish art. This high purpose involves a deep sense of patriotism, a pride created and sustained by past greatness and aroused at seeing Spain's decorative arts undervalued and neglected in favor of the foreign merchandise that has invaded our markets and supplied almost all of our national necessities since the beginning of the XVIII century. And yet true art cannot be created or encouraged by a display of bitterness or protest; true art demands creation. Unfortunately foreign crafts and styles became predominant when Spanish wares were inferior or ceased to be produced.

Certainly we can take great pride and feel very Spanish in viewing the best works of contemporary painters because they have great predecessors in the three most brilliant artists of Spain: El Greco, Velázquez and Goya. But we cannot take much pride, for example, in the ceramics of Alcora, because artistically and technically they represent an imitation of a foreign product—a product that we could not produce as well as foreigners did in the XVIII century.

The problem does not lie in Spanish furniture being inferior to that of other countries. Technically, furniture is produced as well in Spain as in other countries but it is inferior artistically. It is not enough to strive for perfection in the art of furniture, or indeed any branch of the applied arts; we must perfect them all. The art of furniture depends entirely on the existence of other arts. The strong support of a style is what matters, since style is the personality of art. When no national style exists, the decorative arts must live at the expense of the style or styles predominant in other lands.

Creating a national style requires not only will and intelligence, but also great aesthetic sensitivity. Many people believe they possess it because they recognize antiques praised in books, or works by contemporary artists whom cultivated people admire. An aesthetic sense is not formed by knowledge of the past. Anyone can learn the characteristics of a style, but only those of suitable temperament can *feel* its beauty. Many people have perverted their aesthetic sense by using it wrongly or by letting it atrophy for lack of use.

One must look at art directly, not from the special vantage point of history. It has been truly said that in art the natural thing is the point of departure not that of arrival. In all arts—especially the decorative—the past can be the point of departure but never arrival. To dwell in the past is to kill the future of art. The future is life, the past is history and archaeology—things observed rather than created.

The decorative arts also depend on the logic of function—the useful purpose that every building or piece of furniture should fulfill. The principle of usefulness is the seed of all that is modern and original in these arts. Practicality clearly determines the structure of a piece of furniture, and from this its form is born. As the structure is perfected, the form becomes purer and more beautiful; only in this way is an original piece of work created, or an art with a personality of its own.

Next comes decoration. The basic construction is clothed with natural, geometric or free form to achieve maximum beauty. These forms never improve upon the basic structure's elegance, but sometimes they can destroy its beauty and even its purpose; we all know furniture that is useless and clumsy in the name of art.

Popular or folk furniture has a special value in Spain not surpassed by any of the countries of old Russia, or Central Europe. The time is not yet ripe for a thorough study of it.

In the present volume we show many examples of our "folk" furniture, not only because its lively characteristics can serve to show the important features of this art in Spain but also because the forms of those pieces are a source of very original work. Popular art has been enjoying a renaissance in late years and the result of this new interest has been the preservation of many old pieces of furniture, embroidery and ceramics. Some collectors have tried to furnish city houses with examples of this popular art and have found that, transplanted, it looks absurd. One of the most complete collections of folk art is exhibited in the National Museum of Decorative Arts in Madrid.

There has been a belief that popular themes in decoration, as in music, can take the place of true artistic inspiration, but this idea is a sad deception. In decorative art, popular motifs are more difficult to use in an original way than themes taken from nature. Mere copying cannot shape a new art.

NOTES

(1) Also the origin of the commode, a piece of furniture that French artists working in the styles called "Louis" lavishly embellished without losing practical use, or practical convenience, the basis for the great development and wide use that it had in Europe.

(2) Not much that is certain is known about the famous *vargueños* that according to tradition were created in Vargas, a town in the province of Toledo. Certainly in Vargas there is no record of any carpenter's shop or workshop for fashioning this furniture or any other. Possibly the name *Vargueño* came from a work shop in Toledo in the XVI century, whose owner, a master carver and cabinetmaker, was named Vargas. This is what the Toledan ceramist, Don Sebastián Aguado, deduced from ancient accounts.

PLATES
LÁMINAS

I 1. XVII century walnut chair; provincial type decorated with simple carving. The back forms a rudimentary arcade, the arches supported by turned spindles; its development is shown on chairs illustrated in Figures 2 through 9, influenced by Renaissance architecture. In England this style appeared during the reign of Charles I. In France and also in Spain backs were made with a double arcade during the reign of Louis XIII, but they were more elegant, being an urban rather than a provincial art form; their spindles are thinner and the crosspieces more richly decorated.

This crudely constructed piece was made by a farmer or a village carpenter. The back is more carefully wrought so that it might carry decoration which consists of simple chisel cuts, dentils, and three small rectangles. The development and combination of these motifs attests the decorative intuition of the workman who applied them sensibly and without pretention. National Museum of Decorative Arts, Madrid.

2. XVII century provincial style walnut chair. Its decorative elegance is emphasized by the contrast between the back and the rough structure of the frame. Part of the back is reproduced in Plate VII, Figure 19. National Museum of Decorative Arts, Madrid.

3. XVII century provincial walnut chair. This chair is more highly developed and refined than the one reproduced in Figure 1. National Museum of Decorative Arts, Madrid.

LÁMINA I, *fig. 1.*ª - Silla construída en nogal; siglo XVII; tipo popular enriquecido por medio de una talla elemental.

El respaldo afecta la forma rudimentaria de una arquería, sostenidos los arcos por barrotes torneados; su desarrollo en las sillas figuras 2.ª, 3.ª, 4.ª, 5.ª, 6.ª, 7.ª, 8.ª y 9.ª, por influjo arquitectónico del arte del Renacimiento. En Inglaterra aparece ese tipo en el reinado de Carlos I. En Francia se construyen los respaldos con doble arquería (los hay también en España) durante el reinado de Luis XIII, pero con un carácter más elegante al ser de arte suntuoso y no popular; los barrotes son más esbeltos y con más profusión de adornos en los remates.

Es una obra de construcción francamente tosca, hecha indudablemente o por un labriego o por un modesto carpintero de pueblo. Sólo el respaldo está más cuidadosamente trabajado para poder contener una decoración. Como antes se indica, es tan elemental que sólo está formada por sencillos golpes de gubia, unos dentículos y tres pequeños rectángulos. El desarrollo y combinación de esos golpes de gubia y de los dentículos prueba un gran instinto decorador en el modesto artífice, al aplicarlos tan racionalmente y no ser un elemento decorativo de relumbrón.

Museo Nacional de Artes Industriales, de Madrid. - Fotografía de R. Doménech.

LÁMINA I, *fig. 2.*ª - Silla popular construída en nogal; siglo XVII. Elegancia decorativa que resulta más intensa por el contraste del respaldo con la rudeza de la construcción. En la lámina VII, figura 19.ª, se reproduce parte de este respaldo.

Museo Nacional de Artes Industriales, de Madrid. - Fot. de R. Doménech.

LÁMINA I, *fig. 3.*ª - Silla popular construída en nogal; siglo XVII. Es un amplio desarrollo y depuración de formas de la reproducida en la fig. 1.ª

Museo Nacional de Artes Industriales, de Madrid. - Fot. de R. Doménech.

2

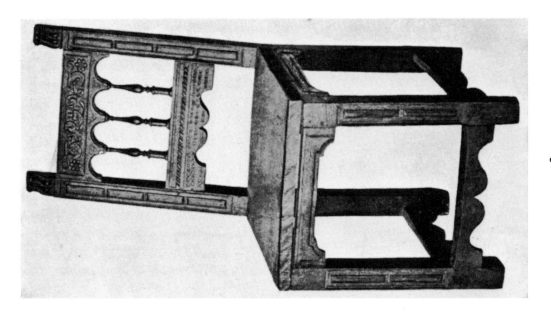

1

3

II

4. XVII century provincial chair. The restraint and success with which only the simplest decorative units have been used gives an impression of elegance that other chairs with more intricate decoration are unable to express. The contrast between simple chisel cuts and other carving gives greater contrasts of light and produces sharper relief effects. National Museum of Decorative Arts, Madrid.

5. XVII century chair. A very robust type of provincial art. A fine example of what can be accomplished by good taste of a child-like quality, with its simple, ingenuous elements, yet achieving great distinction and elegance. National Museum of Decorative Arts, Madrid.

6. XVII century chair, between provincial and urban in style. Similar to the one shown in Figure 1. National Museum of Decorative Arts, Madrid.

LÁMINA II, *fig. 4.ª* - Silla popular del siglo XVII. La sobriedad y el acierto con que se han empleado las unidades decorativas más simples dan una impresión de elegancia que no consiguen expresar otras sillas con un decorado más complejo.

Es de notar el caso que suele repetirse en muchas de esas tallas: de saber contrastar los entalles simplemente grabados, con otros en los que juegan más enérgicamente los contrastes de luz, produciendo mayores efectos de relieve.

Museo Nacional de Artes Industriales, de Madrid.—Fot. de R. Doménech.

LÁMINA II, *fig. 5.ª*—Silla construída en el siglo XVII. Tipo muy recio de arte popular. Magnífico ejemplar de lo que puede dar de sí el buen gusto en un estado verdaderamente infantil, con sus elementos sencillos, ingénuos y con una gran distinción y elegancia en el conjunto.

Museo Nacional de Artes Industriales, de Madrid.—Fot. de R. Doménech.

LÁMINA II, *fig. 6ª*—Silla del siglo XVII. Tipo intermedio de lo popular a lo suntuoso. Véase lo dicho al ocuparnos de la figura 1.ª

Museo Nacional de Artes Industriales, de Madrid.—Fot. de R. Doménech.

6

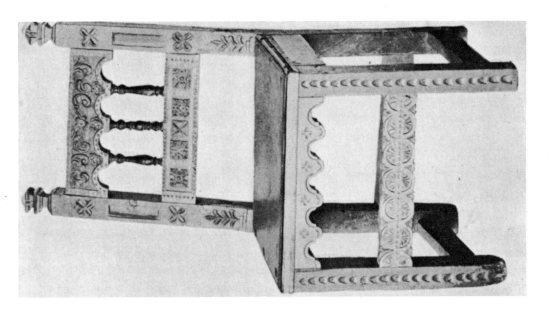

5

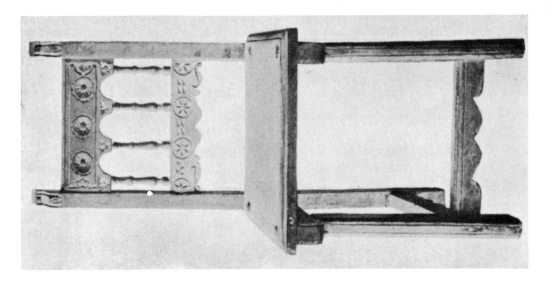

4

III

7. XVII century chair. Between provincial and urban in style. Of fine harmonious proportions yet sturdy; it is profusely decorated without being ornate. The uprights and crosspieces contain a single decorative element: a rosette of four bevelled petals in diagonal form inscribed within a square whose size is regulated by the thickness of the posts and stretchers. A marginal space is allowed on the posts, while on the stretchers a double row of the same rosettes is used, or a simple moulding is added as a border, so that light falls more softly on the concavities than on the angular cuts that form the rosettes. Other features more decorative than essential are added to the crosspieces: arcades upheld by balusters support the back and the seat apron, decorated with leaves and hearts similar to those found on some XVII century Valencian frames. National Museum of Decorative Arts, Madrid.

8. This XVII century walnut chair, structurally more finished than the one shown in Figure 1, retains a distinctly popular character. The artisan has obviously been influenced by architectural decorations and by floral motifs adapted to the circle and the lozenge. The central crest is one of those things seen but not well defined or understood; here it has been translated into an artistically indecisive piece of work. The whole is sober and in good taste. National Museum of Decorative Arts, Madrid.

9. Walnut chair; first third of the XVII century. Markedly influenced by architecture of the period. It is a development of the chair reproduced in Figure 8 with the back terminated in a broken pediment. National Museum of Decorative Arts, Madrid.

LÁMINA III *fig. 7.ª.*—Silla del siglo XVII. Tipo intermedio de lo popular a lo suntuoso. De proporciones elegantes y armoniosas dentro de una gran robustez; está profusamente decorada, sin que dé un efecto recargado. Los largueros y travesaños contienen un solo elemento: la roseta de cuatro hojas biseladas en forma diagonal e inscrita en un cuadrado cuya medida está regulada por los gruesos de dichos largueros y travesaños, dejando un plano marginal en los primeros, invirtiendo en los segundos fajas dobles de las mismas rosetas o una simple moldura, en cuya concavidad juega la luz con más blandura que en los entalles de aristas vivas que forman las rosetas. Asimismo se introducen en esos travesaños otros elementos de más acentuado carácter decorativo que constructivo; unas arquerías sostenidas por balaustres que respaldan el fondo superior y la chambrana delantera, decoradas por unas hojas y rayos de corazón, esbozados en forma análoga a la empleada en bastantes marcos valencianos del siglo XVII.

Museo Nacional de Artes Industriales, de Madrid.—Fot. de R. Doménech.

LÁMINA III, *fig. 8.ª.*— Silla de nogal, siglo XVII.

De técnica constructiva más perfecta que la reproducida en la figura 1.ª, y sin dejar de tener marcado carácter popular, se ve que el artífice al tallarla se sintió influenciado por decoraciones (sobre todo arquitectónicas) que había visto, y por motivos florales adaptados a dos formas alternas, el círculo y el rombo, muy bien elegidos para esa alternancia, formando una faja cortada en sus extremos por los largueros de la silla; pero no constituyen una composición decorativa dentro de ese rectángulo. El remate del centro es uno de esos recuerdos no bien definidos o comprendidos y que se traducen en un trabajo artístico indeciso.

El conjunto es sobrio y de buen gusto.

Museo Nacional de Artes Industriales.—Fot. de R. Doménech.

LÁMINA III, *fig. 9.ª*—Silla en nogal del primer tercio del siglo XVII.

Marcada influencia arquitectónica de la época. Es una transformación de la silla reproducida en la figura 8.ª, rematado el respaldo con un frontón entrecortado.

Museo Nacional de Artes Industriales, de Madrid.—Fot. de R. Doménech.

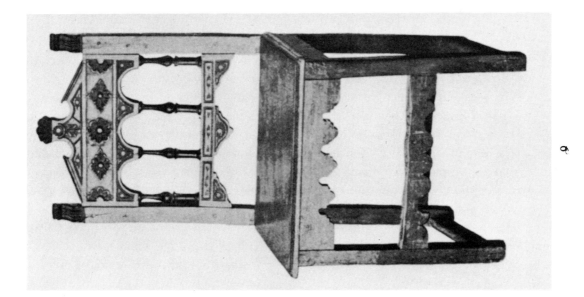

6

8

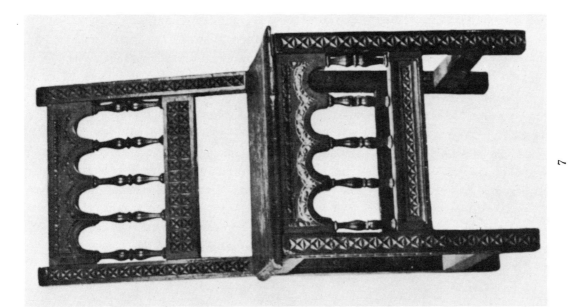

7

IV **10.** XVII century chair. In the Villa Palmieri, in Florence, there is a sumptuous chair with a back divided into two parts, and a row of small arches supported by slender turned spindles. Structurally the back of the Spanish chair shown here has a certain relationship to the Italian type. It is elegant and sober, decorated with themes that are simple yet impressive because of persistent repetition, well proportioned and balanced; that is, the decorative themes have been apportioned so precisely and perfectly that one cannot envision a change that would not destroy the beauty of the composition. National Museum of Decorative Arts, Madrid.

11. Walnut chair built at the end of the XVI or the beginning of the XVII century. If examined piece by piece (see Figure 21), this chair does not produce the impression of beauty that is given by the whole.

The systematic use of chisel cuts forming semi-imbrications on all of the uprights gives the vertical lines of the piece a special quality that contrasts strikingly with the carving used on the horizontals; although both are ornamented with chip carving, the play of light gives more brilliant touches to the verticals so that the result is different. In brief, the appearance of rich work is achieved with an exceedingly simple theme. National Museum of Decorative Arts, Madrid.

12. XVII century chair. This chair and those reproduced in Figures 13 and 14 are closely related. Turning predominates on the chair shown in Figure 12 which is less elegant than the others and somewhat cumbersome, but well realized within this kind of solid form. The arched top splat of the back with two very simple motifs, a shell framed by two spirals, produces a beautiful and original decorative effect. The base of the shell, repeating the spiral and enclosing a rosette, reveals naturalness and freedom in choosing decorative motifs, as well as a sure sense of the final effect. National Museum of Decorative Arts, Madrid.

LÁMINA IV, *fig. 10.ª*—Silla del siglo XVII. En la villa Palmieri, de Florencia, existe una silla muy lujosa, cuyo respaldo está dividido en dos zonas con una faja de arquillos sostenidos por delgados barrotes trabajados a torno. Como estructura general, guarda el respaldo de la silla española cierto parentesco con la italiana. Es un ejemplar suntuoso y sobrio. Una decoración cuyos temas son sencillos y que se imponen por una persistente repetición bien compensada o equilibrada; es decir: esos temas decorativos se han repartido de un modo tan preciso y perfecto que no se concibe un cambio sin destruir la belleza de esa composición.

Museo Nacional de Artes Industriales, de Madrid.—Fot. de R. Doménech.

LÁMINA IV, *fig. 11.ª*—Silla de nogal construída a fines del siglo XVI o comienzos del XVII. Examinada esta silla en detalle (véase la ampliación del respaldo en la fig. 21), no produce la impresión de belleza que en su conjunto.

El empleo sistemático de los golpes de gubia en forma semi-imbricada en todos los largueros, da a las líneas verticales del mueble una calidad especial que contrasta notablemente con la talla empleada en las horizontales; pues si bien la talla en estas últimas piezas de la silla está conseguida a golpes de gubia como en las otras, la luz da más toques brillantes en las verticales y por lo mismo el resultado es distinto. En resumen, un aspecto de trabajo rico con un tema muy rudimentario, sumamente simple.

Museo Nacional de Artes Industriales, de Madrid,—Fot. de R. Doménech.

LÁMINA IV, *fig 12.ª*—Silla del siglo XVII. Esta y las reproducidas en las fig. 13.ª y 14.ª tienen una gran hermandad. En la 12.ª predominan las formas torneadas; ésta es menos elegante que las otras, resulta un tanto pesada, pero bien concebida dentro de ese tipo de solidez. El copete del respaldo, con dos temas tan sencillos como son una concha y dos espiras encuadrándola, produce un hermoso efecto decorativo, bien original. En el arranque de la concha, repetir la espira y encerrar en ella una roseta revela desenfado y libertad en resolver los temas decorativos y al propio tiempo un sentido seguro del resultado.

Museo Nacional de Artes Industriales de Madrid.—Fot. de R. Doménech.

10

11

12

V 13. This Mallorcan chair, from the beginning of the XVIII century, is about the same size as the chair in Figure 14, but seems lighter because of the tapered extremities of its turned posts.

The back is well designed, but the decoration of the top splat is too massive and the silhouette leaves something to be desired. This defect has been toned down a little by the side finials; without them the cresting would be even more prominent. The large circular surface is not justified by the decoration that it contains; the motif is of no value there and too much free space remains. The two turned stretchers below the seat are an unfortunate later addition, made to strengthen the frame. Private Collection. Palma de Mallorca.

14. Mallorcan chair, of the beginning of the XVIII century. This is the most beautiful and elegant of all of the chairs illustrated here, both in general shape and in details. Graceful and well proportioned, its strength is hidden, and therefore not cumbersome. The decoration on the back is adapted perfectly to its shape; an unfolding stylized sunflower of a kind that seems to recall old decorative forms, but that has a marked stamp of original *modernity*. Private Collection. Palma de Mallorca.

15. XVIII century chair. The decorative elements of this chair show a certain Italian influence but the frame is Spanish. The stylized butterfly at the center of the back displays a childlike flight of imagination; the same is true of the other details of the back, although the small central fleuron at the crest and the design of the seat apron and front stretcher reveal a more sophisticated technique. National Museum of Decorative Arts, Madrid.

LÁMINA V, *fig. 13.ª* - Silla de tipo levantino (mallorquín) de comienzos del siglo XVIII. Su proporción es muy semejante a la reproducida en la figura 14.ª y aun parece más ligera por los entrantes de los balaustres torneados.

El respaldo está bien compuesto, aunque el remate resulte sobrado voluminoso y la silueta sea poco agradable; válgale el haber atenuado un tanto ese defecto con los pomos laterales, pues de no ser así, se acusaría mucho la masa circular. Este gran plano circular no está perfectamente justificado por la decoración que contiene: el motivo está allí muy holgado y queda sobrado espacio libre. Este motivo resulta verdaderamente original, pero algo híbrido y amazacotado; el grupo de la base, o sea el que recibe el círculo, está mucho mejor resuelto, es más lógico, si bien la solución es elementalísima.

Col. particular en Palma de Mallorca.—Fotografía del Arx. Mas.

LÁMINA V, *fig. 14.ª* - Silla de tipo levantino (Mallorca) de comienzos del siglo XVIII. Es un ejemplar bellísimo y el más elegante de cuantos se reproducen, tanto en sus formas generales como en la solución de los detalles.

Es esbelta y bien proporcionada, con lo cual disimula su robustez, que no llega, por esto, a ser pesada. La decoración del respaldo se adapta perfectamente a la forma: en el remate se desarrolla un girasol admirablemente estilizado, con un carácter que parece recordar formas decorativas lejanas, pero que tiene un gran sello de *modernidad* por lo original que es.

Los travesaños de la parte baja son postizos hechos en una desdichadísima restauración.

Col. particular, en Palma de Mallorca.—Fotografía del Arx. Mas.

LÁMINA V, *fig. 15.ª* - Silla del siglo XVIII. Hay en ese mueble una cierta influencia italiana en los elementos decorativos; el armazón es español. La mariposa del centro del respaldo es de una valentía verdaderamente infantil en su estilización y lo mismo ocurre con los demás detalles del respaldo, si bien el pequeño florón central en la parte superior y la traza y talla de la chambrana y delantera del asiento acusan una técnica más sabia.

Museo Nacional de Artes Industriales, de Madrid.—Fot. de R. Doménech.

15

14

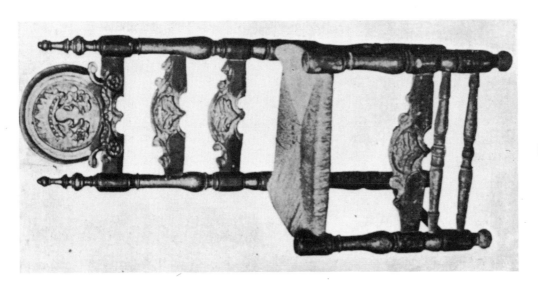

13

VI 16. Spanish walnut chair, second half of the XVI century. An extraordinarily rare type, with a distinctive provincial character. The back—balusters as well as crosspieces—is executed with fine decorative logic and novelty to achieve a beautiful effect with simple rustic elements. National Museum of Decorative Arts, Madrid. 17. XVI century walnut chair. This example may be considered a rich and more sophisticated development of the one illustrated in Figure 16. The decorations on the back are the same; the pediment-like cresting varies, and the balusters that support the arches are replaced by a band of inverted arches that form hollow circles.

National Museum of Decorative Arts, Madrid. 18. XVII century armchair. A provincial interpretation of an urban type of the same period. Its strange appearance results from the contrast between the refined lines and shapes of the original type and the rough interpretation of the provincial craftsman. The back, with a delicately cut out vase in the center and slender vertical splints resembling open fan sticks filling up the hollows, shows a certain indecision in its translation into popular technique, but the original design is still recognizable. National Museum of Decorative Arts, Madrid.

LÁMINA VI, *fig. 16.ª* - Silla española construída en nogal, en la segunda mitad del siglo XVI.

Tipo extraordinariamente raro, de un marcadísimo carácter popular. La composición del respaldo, tanto en los balaustres como en las fajas, es de una lógica decorativa tan grande y de una novedad tan saliente, que con elementos tan sencillos y rústicos se ha conseguido un efecto muy bello.

Museo Nacional de Artes Industriales, de Madrid.—Fot. de R. Doménech.

LÁMINA VI, *fig. 17.ª* - Silla del siglo XVI, construída en nogal. Puede considerarse este ejemplar como un rico y más sabio desarrollo del reproducido en el grabado anterior. Los elementos decorativos del respaldo son los mismos; varía el copete a modo de frontón y se substituyen los balaustres que sostienen los arquillos por otra faja igual invertida, dando lugar a círculos en hueco.

LÁMINA VI, *fig. 18.ª* - Sillón del siglo XVII. Interpretación popular de un tipo suntuoso de la misma época; esto le da un aspecto extraño, estableciéndose un fuerte contraste entre la delicadeza de líneas y formas del tipo primitivo y la interpretación ruda de lo popular.

Aquellos respaldos calados frágilmente con un jarrón en el centro y delgadas tablillas en rectas o curvas caprichosas para rellenar los huecos formando una especie de varillaje de abanico, traducidos a la técnica popular dieron por resultado cierta indecisión, pero a través de todo no puede por menos de distinguirse el tipo original.

Obsérvese la relación decorativa tan estrecha en el modo de estar compuestas la parte alta y la baja del respaldo y cómo en la primera se substituye la roseta por el águila bicéfala, otro elemento de arte sabio que adopta el modesto ebanista del pueblo.

Museo Nacional de Artes Industriales, de Madrid.—Fot. de R. Doménech.

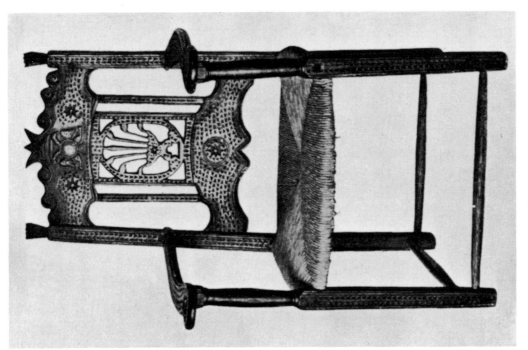

18

17

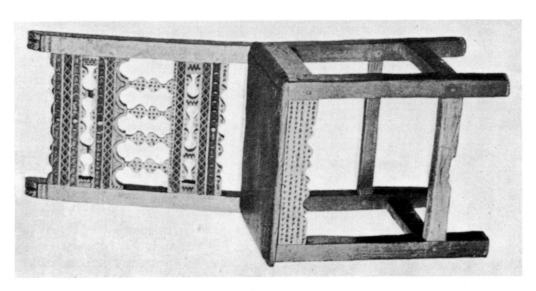

16

VII

19, 20. Backs of chairs reproduced in Figures 2 and 7.

LÁMINA VII, *figs. 19.ª y 20.ª* - Respaldos de las sillas reproducidas en las figuras 2.ª y 7.ª.

19

20

VIII

21, 22. Backs of chairs reproduced in Figures 11 and 17. The general plan of the composition of the chair in Figure 22 is as simple as the units comprising it. It is divided into a series of parallel bands of the same width when carved, and double width when pierced. The effect does not become monotonous because the bands with chip carving are contrasted with bands decorated with slightly rounded petals. Light falls differently on each one of these bands, and on the pierced-work where shapes and size produce the same effect but with a different, stronger accent, preventing the decoration on the back from seeming too detailed.

LÁMINA VIII, *figs. 21.ª y 22.ª* - Respaldos de las sillas reproducidas en las figuras núms. 11.ª y 17.ª

El plan general de la composición tiene la misma simplicidad que el de las unidades empleadas. Aquélla se reduce a una serie de fajas paralelas, de anchura semejante en las correspondientes a las tallas y doble en las de los calados; sin que resulte monótono el total, por estar admirablemente contrastadas las fajas con tallas a bisel, de las otras fajas formadas por hojas ligeramente redondeadas en sus planos, mediante lo cual juega la luz de modo muy diferente en cada una de esas fajas, así como en los calados, cuyas formas y magnitudes producen los mismos efectos, pero en una acentuación muy enérgica, quitando migrosidad al conjunto decorativo del respaldo.

Museo Nacional de Artes Industriales, de Madrid.—Fot. de R. Doménech.

21

22

IX

23. XVI century armchair. This and Figure 24 are purely Spanish. The similarities to those that were constructed in Italy, France, England, Germany, and the Low Countries during the XVI and XVII centuries are due to Spanish influence. In this period our workshops exported a great number of these simple, large and comfortable pieces to other European countries, where they became popular. The chair has a pierced stretcher. A. Paramo Collection, Madrid.

24. XVI century armchair. The front stretcher is richly carved and the velvet on the back and seat has silk fringe and gilded nail heads. It is one of the finest examples of the period. Private Collection.

Lámina IX, *fig. 23.ª* - Sillón del siglo XVI. Este y los siguientes son netamente españoles. Las semejanzas que tienen los construídos en los siglos XVI y XVII en Italia, Francia, Inglaterra, Alemania y Países Bajos, es por influencia española. En esa época nuestros talleres producían para una gran exportación a los países de Europa. Esas formas sencillas, grandiosas y cómodas se impusieron en el extranjero.

Tiene este sillón la chambrana calada.

Col. A. Páramo, Madrid.—Fot. de R. Doménech.

Lámina IX, *fig. 24.ª* - Sillón del siglo XVI. Chambrana ricamente tallada y los terciopelos del respaldo y asiento con flecos de sedería y clavazón dorada. Representa uno de los ejemplares más suntuosos de esa época.

Col. particular.—Fot. de J. Roig.

24

23

X

25. XVI century monk's chair enriched by carving on the front stretcher and by figured velvet upholstery on the leather back and seat. C. March Collection, Palma de Mallorca.

26. XVI century armchair. The silhouette is more refined than that of the previous chair, to which it is very similar. City Hall, Palma de Mallorca.

LÁMINA X, *fig. 25.*ª - Sillón del siglo XVI, tipo frailero enriquecido con la talla de la chambrana y el sobrepuesto de un tejido de terciopelo labrado sobre los cueros del respaldo y asiento.

Col. C. March, Palma de Mallorca.—Fot. del Arx. Mas.

LÁMINA X, *fig. 26.*ª - Sillón del siglo XVI. Más refinado su esqueleto que el del sillón anterior, con el que guarda bastante semejanza.

Casa de la Ciudad de Palma de Mallorca.—Fotografía del Arx. Mas.

XI

27. Armchair from the end of the XVI or the beginning of the XVII century. This style of furniture was fashioned by Catalan and Aragonese turners during this period; it was also made in Portugal. The sobriety of straight lines, so typically Spanish, has been lost. National Museum of Decorative Arts, Madrid.

28. XVII century armchair of the same style as Figure 27, but its elegance and fine proportions show the Louis XIII influence. Private Collection.

LÁMINA XI, *fig. 27.ª* - Sillón de fines del siglo XVI o comienzos del XVII. Tipo del mobiliario en trabajos torneados catalanes y aragoneses de esa época; también se produjeron en Portugal. Se ha perdido la sobriedad de las líneas rectas, tan netamente españolas.

Museo Nacional de Artes Industriales.—Fotografía de R. Doménech.

LÁMINA XI, *fig. 28.ª* - Sillón del siglo XVII, del mismo tipo que el anterior; pero por su elegancia y bellas proporciones denota una influencia del estilo de Luís XIII.

Col. particular.—Fot. de J. Roig.

28

27

XII

29. Armchair from the last third of the XVII century. An uncommon type of Spanish workmanship. The carving is influenced by French work. March Collection, Palma de Mallorca.

LÁMINA XII, *fig. 29.ª* - Sillón del último tercio del siglo XVII, tipo poco corriente; trabajo español. La talla es de influencia francesa.

Col. March, de Palma de Mallorca.—Fot. del Arx. Mas.

29

XIII

30. XIV–XV century Hispano-Moresque coffret of fine wood with polychrome intarsia. The rich or elaborate appearance of inlaid *vargueños* and boxes is the total effect of an extensive, well-balanced piece of work against very plain surfaces. These surfaces always have a simple decorative scheme: a spatial rhythm of repetition and alternation in a regular pattern. The motifs thus become perfectly legible, and their components make a pleasant impression that enhances the effect of decorative richness. This is more illusory than real, since often the decorative units are poor in themselves, but the way they are used results in profusion and effectiveness. This decorative principle has governed the ornament of many pieces of furniture besides the coffret shown here. Private Collection.

LÁMINA XIII, *fig. 30.ª* - Cofrecillo hispanoárabe del siglo XIV al XV. Armazón de madera fina recubierta de taraceas policromadas.

La impresión de cosa rica o suntuosa que suelen producir los vargueños y arquillas taraceados, está conseguida por el conjunto que da un trabajo considerable, bien coordinado sobre planos muy simples. Estos planos reciben siempre una decoración igualmente sencilla, organizada mediante ritmos de espacios en que casi siempre juegan, en forma constante, la repetición y la alternación. Así resultan perfectamente *legibles* los motivos, y al comprenderse con tanta facilidad, sus componentes dan una impresión de placer que favorece al concepto de la riqueza decorativa; siendo esa impresión más aparente que real, pues en el fondo no hay tal riqueza, toda vez que las unidades decorativas pueden ser pobres; lo que hay, es profusión y acierto en su empleo. Ese principio decorativo es el que ha regido en la composición decorativa de muchos muebles, entre ellos el cofrecillo que se reproduce en la figura 30.ª

Col. particular.—Fot. de J. Roig.

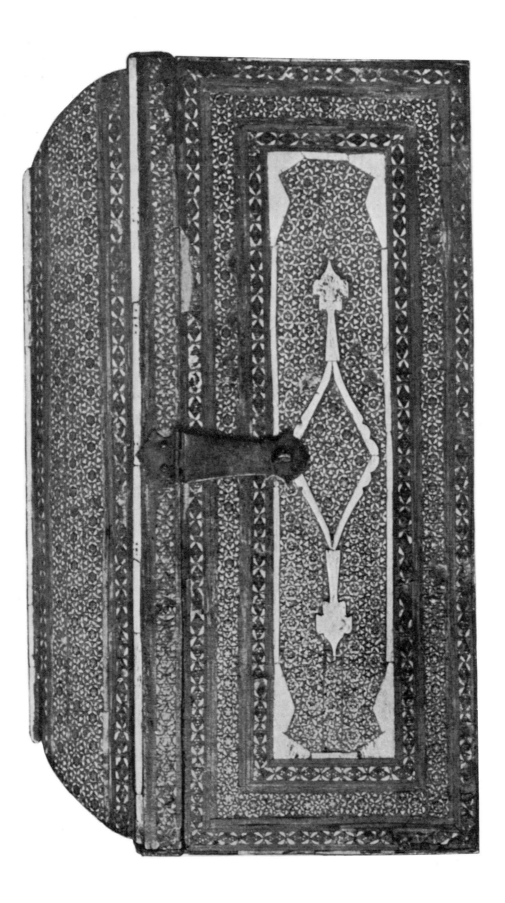

XIV

31. Small XV century Spanish *mudéjar* chest, decorated with geometric tracery inlaid in ivory. This style, with deviations, principally structural, lasted throughout the XVI and part of the XVII century. The mosaic work is composed of bits of ivory or bone stained or artificially colored, and skillfully arranged in multiple combinations of geometric elements. The design is also worked out with pieces of natural-colored or stained wood, a result of the influence of the Italian intarsia work that predominated from the beginning of the XVI century. Eventually Italian intarsia work abandoned geometric elements, formed compositions based on flora and fauna, and finally became almost pictorial. Private Collection.

LÁMINA XIV, *fig. 31.ª* - Arquilla española, estilo mudéjar del siglo XV. Trabajo de tracerías poligonales ejecutado en taracea de marfil.

Este tipo se continuó repitiendo con variantes, principalmente en los ángulos y uniones, durante el siglo XVI y parte del XVII. Realmente es el trabajo en mosaico ejecutado con trozos de marfil o de hueso teñidos o coloridos artificialmente, para hacer juego con múltiples combinaciones de elementos geométricos. Esas materias también se combinaron con trozos de maderas de colores naturales o teñidas; esto último por influencia del arte italiano que predominó desde los comienzos del siglo XVI y es insuperable en las labores de tarsia, que abandonando los elementos geométricos, realizó composiciones a base de unidades de flora y de fauna, hasta llegar a ejecutar casi cuadros.

Respecto a la técnica decorativa de este mueble, véase lo dicho en el anterior.

Col. particular.—Fot. de J. Roig.

31

XV

32. Chest of fine wood richly decorated with minute designs in ivory inlay. Although the chest is of XVI century Spanish workmanship, nearly all of the designs were inspired by Oriental compositions.

The most striking motifs in the decoration on this chest are the three large rosettes on the front panels, inlaid in the *mudéjar* style. The central one seems to be inspired by the geometric tracery of Arabic tiles, and the other two more by cross-stitch embroidery, in which *mudéjar* interlacing is seen in the arabesques of the plain background. The horizontal bands of the chest lack pronounced individuality; except for the widest, whose decorative composition is not well solved, the individual motifs have no relationship to each other. Lázaro Collection.

LÁMINA XV, *fig. 32.*ª - Arca de maderas finas ricamente decorada con menuda labor de taracea en marfil. Trabajo español del siglo XVI, inspirados casi todos sus temas decorativos en composiciones orientales.

Lo más notable de la ornamentación de esta arca son los tres grandes rosetones de los paneles centrales hechos con taracea a la manera mudéjar. El del centro parece inspirado en la tracería poligonal de los azulejos árabes y los otros dos parecen más bien originados por bordados a punto cruzado en que se notan las lacerías mudéjares en los arabescos formados por los planos del fondo, más que en el dibujo embutido de los mismos. Las fajas no ofrecen particularidad saliente; sólo la más ancha, que por su composición decorativa que no está bien solucionada, quedan las unidas sueltas, sin trabazón.

Col. Lázaro.—Fot. de J. Roig.

XVI

33. Box of fine wood and ivory inlay; end of the XVI or beginning of the XVII century. A type characteristic of the Mediterranean basin showing Italian influence. Property of the Marquesa de la Cénia, Palma de Mallorca.

LÁMINA XVI, *fig. 33.ª* - Caja de maderas finas y taracea de marfil; trabajo de fines del siglo XVI o principios del XVII. Tipo propio de la cuenca mediterránea; se ven en esa obra influencias italianas.
Propiedad de la Excma. Sra. Marquesa de la Cénia, en Palma de Mallorca.—Fot. del Arx. Mas.

33

XVII

34. Cabinet decorated with ivory inlay, end of the XVI century, perhaps made in Granada. Decorative units in the Hispano-Moresque tradition, strongly influenced by tilemakers. The profiles of the mouldings are well solved, and the designs on the doors at either side are as ingenious as they are beautiful. Lázaro Collection.

LÁMINA XVII, *fig. 34.*ª - Arquimesa decorada con taraceas de marfil; fines del siglo XVI, tal vez ejecutada en Granada. Unidades decorativas de tradición oriental arábigomorisca, con marcada influencia de la azulejería. El trazado de las molduras está sabiamente resuelto y las dos composiciones laterales son tan ingeniosas como bellas. *Col. Lázaro.—Fot. de J. Roig.*

34

XVIII

35. *Papelera* with delicate inlaid decoration. The central section is made in the shape of a portal and the piece shows Italian influence. From the end of the XVI or the beginning of the XVII century. Lázaro Collection.

Lamina XVIII, *fig. 35.*ª - Caja papelera con decoración de taracea, de finísima labor; centro resuelto al modo de una portada arquitectónica; influencia italiana. Trabajo de fines del siglo XVI o comienzos del XVII.

Col. *Lázaro.—Fot. J. Roig.*

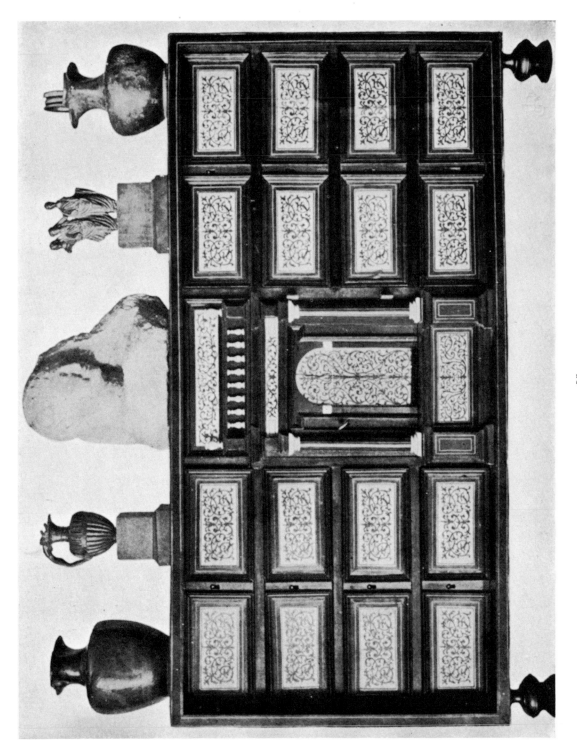

XIX

36. XVII century inlaid cabinet. Italian influence can be detected in some of the decorative compositions. The decoration is much better in detail than on the whole, since in too many cases the motifs are joined with the framing designs. The framework is noteworthy because it is decorated in very simple patterns whose straight lines contrast with the curvilinear forms on almost all of the panels; but that, if one looks sidewise at the small ones, they form a gray mass. On the large panels the decorations are better spaced. Private Collection, Palma de Mallorca.

LÁMINA XIX *fig. 36.ª* - Arquimesa del siglo XVII; decoración de taraceas; influencia italiana, según puede observarse en algunas de las composiciones decorativas. Está mucho mejor resuelta en detalle que en conjunto, pues se unen demasiado los motivos decorativos con los que vienen a encuadrarlos; valga el que, en estos últimos, se emplean siempre unidades rectilíneas muy simples, que contrastan con las formas curvilíneas de los motivos decorativos de casi todos los paneles; pero, así y todo, nótese en los pequeños, si se entorna la vista, que resultan una masa gris. En los paneles grandes están mejor espaciados los elementos decorativos.

Col. particular, en Palma de Mallorca.—Fotografía del Arx. Mas.

36

XX

37. XVII century *papelera* with drawers and inlaid front on an arcaded trestle stand. The designs show Italian influence. The drawers are very well spaced; the side doors, reduced a third more than the center drawers, break the monotony of a uniform set of pigeon holes and allow the upper and lower drawers of the side rows to be equal in size. Barcelona Museum.

LÁMINA XX, *fig. 37.ª* - Arquilla papelera con cajonería, decorados sus frentes con taraceas. Composiciones de influencia italiana; pie de arquería o de puente; siglo XVII. La cajonería está muy bien distribuída; las puertecitas laterales, bajando un tercio más que los cajones del centro, rompen la monotonía de un encasillado uniforme y permite que se correspondan los tamaños superior e inferior de las hiladas laterales.
Museo de Barcelona.—Fot. del Arx. Mas.

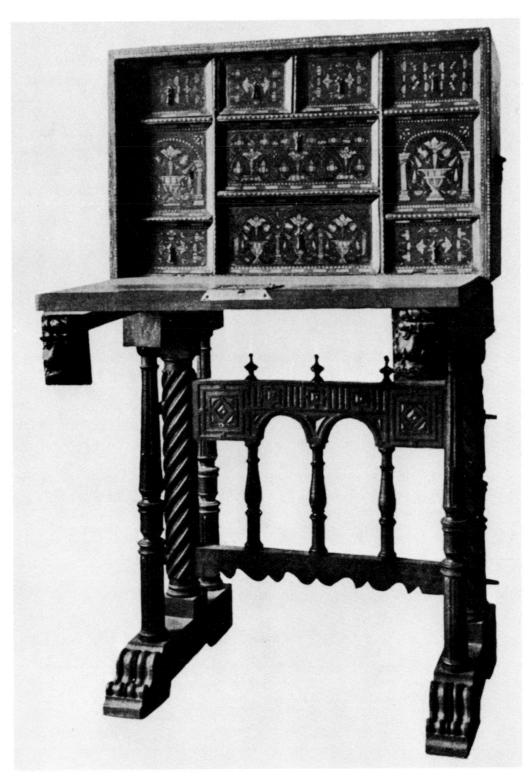

37

XXI

38. Small XV century chest. The sides and top are carved. The designs on the cover are sometimes seen in embroideries of the last third of the XV and the beginning of the XVI century; frequently these carvings are gilded and painted.

Lámina XXI, *fig. 38.*ª - Arquilla del siglo xv. Los frentes y tapa van tallados; los elementos decorativos de la tapa se ven algunas veces en los bordados del último tercio del siglo xv y principios del xvi; con frecuencia esos trabajos de talla van dorados y policromados.

38

XXII

39. Chest, end of the XV century. The carving at the front in the upper part, with rosettes inscribed within lozenges, has the same theme as wooden ceilings of the period, either with the wood in natural color or its projections polychromed or gilded. The lower part is made into a blind arcade, a decorative theme used on many XV century buildings. Lázaro Collection.

LÁMINA XXII, *fig. 39*ª - Arca de fines del siglo xv. La talla de su frente acusa en la faja superior, con los florones inscritos en los cuadriláteros, el mismo tema de los artesonados de esa época, bien con la madera en su propio color, o policromados y dorados sus pujantes. La faja inferior formada por una falsa arquería, es tema decorativo usado en muchos edificios del siglo xv.

Col. Lázaro. - Fot. de J. Roig.

39

XXIII

40. Cabinet, first half of the XVI century. The Gothic feeling lingers in the minute design of the carving. The stand is arcaded. Lázaro Collection.

Lámina XXIII, *fig. 40.*ª - Arquimesa de la primera mitad del siglo XVI. En la menuda labor de talla perdura el sentido decorativo gótico. El pie es de arquería.

Col. Lázaro. - Fot. J. Roig.

XXIV

41. Detail of the preceding cabinet.

Lámina xxiv, *fig. 41.*ª - Ampliación de la arquimesa anterior.

41

XXV

42. *Papelera* with double lid (front and top), the background and drawers carved in low relief. Typical example of the XV or beginning of the XVI century. Private Collection.

Lámina XXV, *fig. 42.*ª - Arquilla papelera de doble tapa (frente y cubierta) fondo y cajonería tallados en bajo relieve. Ejemplar tipo siglo XVI o comienzos del XVII.

Col. particular. - Fot. de J. Roig.

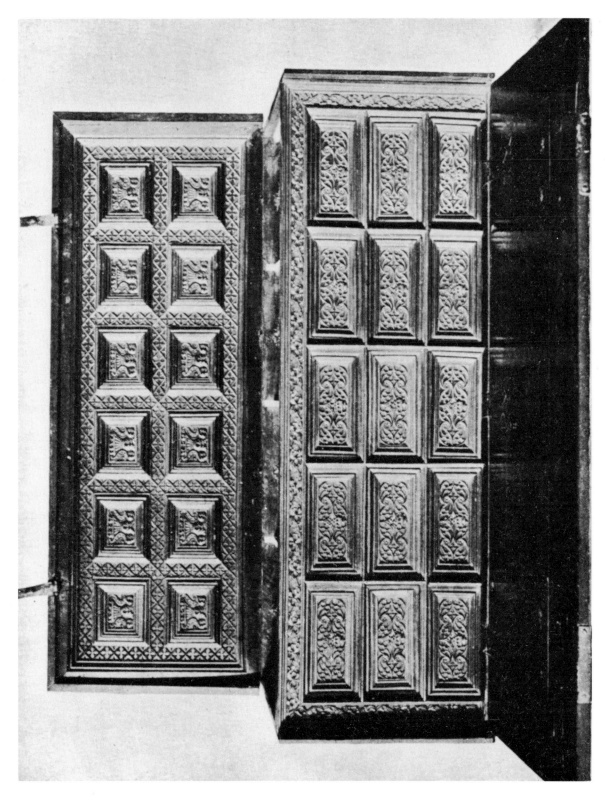

XXVI

43. *Vargueño* with trestle stand. A typical example from the XVI century. Lázaro Collection.

LÁMINA XXVI, *fig. 43.*ª - Caja vargueño con pie de puente. Ejemplo tipo del siglo XVI.

Col. Lázaro. - Fot. de J. Roig.

43

XXVII

44. XVI century *vargueño* with cabinet base. This is one of the most splendid examples of Spanish cabinetwork. Without architectural pretensions, as in the pieces reproduced in Figures 46 and 51, and without copying the attenuated form in Figure 50, this *vargueño* is an example of the ideal fusion of architecture and decoration. This piece of furniture cannot be criticized as "minor architecture." On each compartment of the upper body are architectural elements which, except for the colonettes, blind arches and broken pediments, are conceived and fashioned with the simple techniques of the cabinetmaker. Lázaro Collection.

LÁMINA XXVII, *fig. 44.*ª - Contador vargueño con pie de cajonería; siglo XVI. Es uno de los ejemplares más suntuosos y bellos de cuantos ha producido el arte español.

Sin pretensiones arquitectónicas, como en los muebles reproducidos en las figuras núms. 46 y 51 y sin llegar siquiera a la forma atenuada del grabado núm. 50, encontramos en este vargueño un ejemplo de la fusión de la arquitectura y la decoración propiamente dicha.

En ese mueble no se ve el criterio de «arquitectura menor», que engendró tantos desatinos; vemos en cada compartimento del cuerpo superior elementos arquitectónicos en los que, salvo las columnitas, las falsas arquerías y pequeños frontones partidos, todo está pensado y hecho con la sencillez técnica del mueble, y aun esos elementos arquitectónicos antes citados, están tan unidos al resto decorativo del mueble, que se presentan como una acentuación de masas de él, admirablemente repartidas en el centro y laterales bajas.

Col. Lázaro. - Fot. de J. Roig.

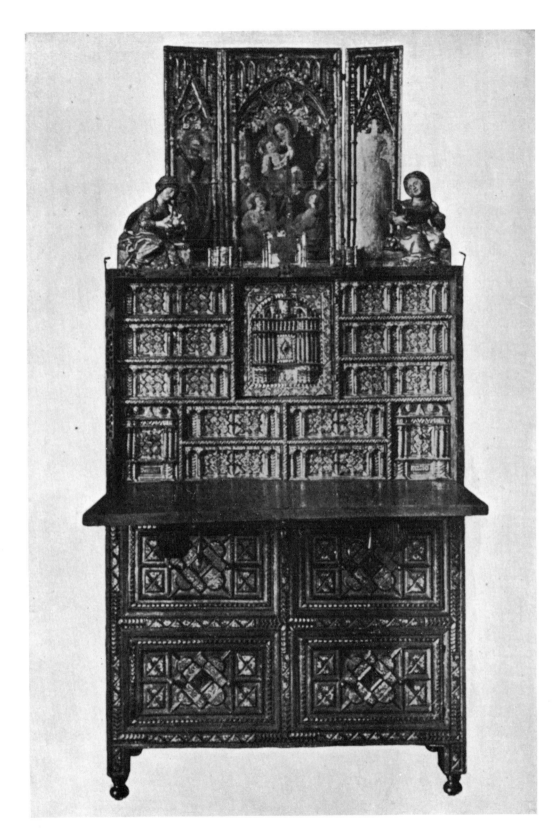

XXVIII

45. *Vargueño* with trestle stand; the drawers are painted and gilded, with colonettes of turned bone. Typical of the last third of the XVI century. The decorative treatment of the cabinet is similar to that of the *vargueño* shown in the previous illustration. Zaforteza Collection, Palma de Mallorca.

LÁMINA XXVIII, *fig. 45*.ª - Caja vargueño con pie de puente; cajonería policromada y dorada, con columnillas de hueso, torneadas. Tipo del último tercio del siglo XVI. La caja ofrece grandes analogías de técnica decorativa con la del vargueño reproducido en la lámina anterior.

Col. Zaforteza, de Palma de Mallorca. - Fot. del Arx. Mas.

45

XXIX

46. XVI century cabinet with sculpture in high relief in a style called "Charles the Fifth." Unrestored examples are very rare. This piece has a strong architectural quality, more in its structure than in its decoration, because the carved figures along the sides break the most fundamental lines of the cabinet, especially the upper story. The fronts of the two stories show more restraint and elegance. Fine Arts Museum, Barcelona.

LÁMINA XXIX, *fig. 46.*ª - Contador con esculturas en alto relieve; siglo XVI; tipo llamado de Carlos V. Son muy raros los ejemplares puros y completos que han llegado hasta nosotros.

Tiene ese mueble un marcado carácter arquitectónico, mejor entendido en la traza constructiva que en la decoración, especialmente en las figuras de los costados que rompen las líneas más fundamentales y quitan gallardía al mueble; ese defecto se acentúa en el segundo cuerpo. Las partes centrales de los dos están resueltas con más seriedad y elegancia.

Museo de Bellas Artes de Barcelona. - Fot. del Arx. Mas.

46

XXX

47. *Papelera* on trestle stand. The drawers are decorated with delicate, highly-styled inlay in floral themes. Typical work of the XVI–XVII century, showing Italian influence. Lázaro Collection.

LÁMINA XXX, *fig. 47.*ª - Caja papelera; cajonería decorada con finísima taracea de temas florales muy estilizados; labor propia del siglo XVI; persiste hasta muy avanzado el siglo XVII. Influencia italiana. Pie de puente.

Col. Lázaro. - Fot. de J. Roig.

47

XXXI

48. XVI century papelera on an arcaded trestle *vargueño* stand. Enlarged on the next plate. Private Collection.

Lámina XXXI, *fig. 48.ª* - Caja papelera y pie de arquería del tipo vargueño; siglo XVI. Se amplía en la lámina siguiente.

Col. particular. - Fot. de J. Roig

48

XXXII

49. Enlarged view of the *papelera* in Figure 48.

LÁMINA XXXII, *fig. 49.ª* - Ampliación de la figura anterior.

49

XXXIII

50. XVII century cabinet with an architectural door at the center and drawers at the sides. The cabinet and the table are decorated with carvings and applications of gilded bronze, and inlay of the same metal. Private Collection.

LÁMINA XXXIII, *fig. 50.ª* - Arquimesa con portada de tipo arquitectónico en el centro y cajonería a los lados. Decoración con esculturas y aplicaciones de bronce dorado a fuego e incrustaciones del mismo metal. La mesa corresponde al mismo tipo del mueble; siglo XVII.

Col. particular. - Fot. de J. Roig.

50

XXXIV

51. XVII century cabinet with center designed architecturally and drawers at the sides decorated with shell plaques, figurines and applications of gilded bronze. The less architectural parts show the most logical decoration; the central section is completely arbitrary in both workmanship and design, since the exterior gives a false impression of the structure. Private Collection.

LÁMINA XXXIV, *fig. 51.ª* - Arquimesa con centro arquitectónico y cajonería a los lados, decorada con placas de concha, figurillas y aplicaciones de bronce dorado a fuego. Siglo XVII.

La parte menos arquitectónica es la de solución más lógica; el cuerpo central es por completo arbitrario en la técnica del mueble y como traza arquitectónica, pues acusa al exterior una estructura completamente falsa.

Col. particular. - Fot. de J. Roig.

51

XXXV

52. Cabinet with XVI century carvings; Spanish adaptation of Renaissance design. All of the carvings are of the same period, but their variety and the arbitrary way the design is composed rouses suspicion that not all of the parts were built for this piece. Private Collection.

Lámina xxxv, *fig. 52.ª* - Arquimesa con tallas del siglo xvi, tipo de adaptación española de la decoración del Renacimiento. Todas las tallas son de la misma época, pero su variedad y lo arbitrario en el modo de estar compuesta la decoración de ese mueble hace suponer que no todas son las que tuvo al ser construído.

Col. particular. - Fot. de J. Roig.

52

XXXVI

53. XVII century cabinet. The carving on the drawers shows French influence. This piece is a good example of how a simple and beautiful composition can be achieved with a single decorative theme. Lázaro Collection.

LÁMINA XXXVI, *fig. 53.ª* - Arquimesa del siglo XVII. La talla de la cajonería es de influencia francesa. Ese mueble presenta un excelente ejemplo de cómo puede conseguirse una composición sencilla y bella con un solo tema decorativo.
Col. Lázaro. - Fot. de J. Roig.

53

XXXVII

54. XVII century *papelera* with drawers decorated in low relief. Private Collection.

Lámina xxxvii, *fig. 54.ª* - Caja papelera; frente de cajonería, con decoración en bajo relieve; siglo xvii.

Col. particular. - Fot. de J. Roig.

54

XXXVIII

55. Small chest inlaid with fine wood and ivory, typical of Spanish work of the late XVII century, showing Italo-Flemish influence. Its decoration is ineffectual because the decorative bands are all of the same width. Private Collection.

LÁMINA XXXVIII, *fig. 55.ª* - Arquilla de maderas finas y taraceas de marfil; pieza propia del mobiliario español de fines del siglo XVII; influencia italoflamenca. La decoración resulta de una marcada sequedad, perjudicándole la insistencia de un mismo ancho de las fajas decorativas.
Col. particular. - Fot. de J. Roig.

55

XXXIX

56. Large carved walnut chest of the early XVII century. The decorative motifs of this period, showing Italian influence, were often made in Eastern Spain and other countries along the Mediterranean basin. The smaller piece is a XVI century *mudéjar*-style cedar coffret. On the cover is the following inscription: "I belong to Doña Catalina de Omes and was made in her name."

LÁMINA XXXIX, *fig. 56.ª* - Arca grande, construída en nogal, con trabajos de talla del primer tercio del siglo XVII. Los motivos decorativos son muy frecuentes en los trabajos de esa época, ejecutados en la región levantina española y gran parte de la cuenca mediterránea, por influencia italiana.

El mueble pequeño es una arquilla en madera de cedro, tipo mudéjar del siglo XVI. En la tapa hay la siguiente inscripción: *Soy de Doña Catalina de Omes y en su nombre se hizo.*

Museo Nacional de Artes Industriales. - Fot. de R. Doménech.

56

XL

57. Walnut chest with XVII century carving very typical of the Spanish Levant and the Balearic Islands. The placement of blind arches against a smooth background gives a clear and restful effect despite the richness of the decoration. National Museum of Decorative Arts, Madrid.

LÁMINA XL, *fig. 57.ª* - Arca de nogal. Trabajo en talla del siglo XVII, muy peculiar del Levante español y frecuentemente de las islas Baleares. La disposición de las falsas arquerías dejando lisos sus fondos, deja la composición clara y tranquila a pesar de la riqueza decorativa que tiene.

Museo Nacional de Artes industriales. - Fot. de R. Doménech.

57

XLI

58. XVII century carved chest. March Collection, Palma de Mallorca.

LÁMINA XLI, *fig. 58.ª* - Arca decorada con tallas del siglo XVII.

Col. March, de Palma de Mallorca. - Fot. del Arx. Mas.

58

58

XLII

59. XVII century chest. The decoration shows the persistence of ancient motifs, so well rooted that they lasted until the XIX century. The whole design is magnificent. Decoration is done in chip carving, so typical of folk art in all countries. National Museum of Decorative Arts, Madrid.

LÁMINA XLII, *fig. 59.ª* - Arcón del siglo XVII. Los motivos decorativos de las tallas manifiestan la persistencia de unidades empleadas en siglos anteriores, y tal arraigo tienen, que han persistido hasta el siglo XIX. El conjunto está compuesto con grandiosidad. Los motivos decorativos resueltos en talla de forma biselada, tan característica en el arte popular de todos los países.

Museo Nacional de Artes Industriales. - Fot. de R. Doménech.

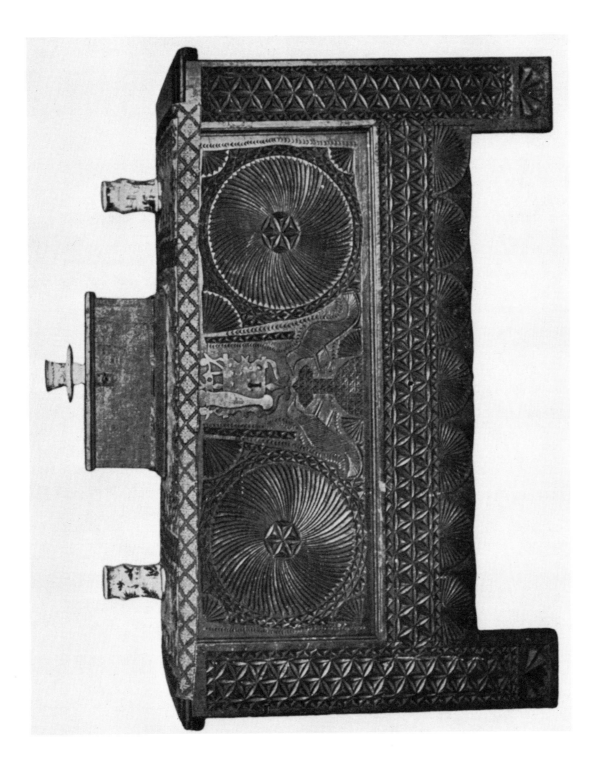

XLIII

60. XVII century provincial chest. The very conventional decorative elements of this piece produce a fresh effect because of the way they are distributed and handled. The plain surfaces are well arranged and the carving is strong. The composition of the front demonstrates perfect structural logic: the sides retain the quality of simple uprights, dramatizing the wider dimension of the base, whose decoration is on a smaller scale, but perfectly proportioned to the decorative themes of the center thus establishing an adequate separation of the container and the contained. The central panel, with the symbol of the Sacrament and the theme of rosettes, is decorated with great sobriety, and its solemnity seems to strengthen the spiritual force of this symbol. This piece is another example of folk art derived from a more elaborate and sophisticated artistic tradition. Private Collection, Palma de Mallorca.

LÁMINA XLIII, *fig. 60.ª* - Arcón tipo popular del siglo XVII.

Los elementos decorativos que forman la composición de ese mueble son muy usuales, y, sin embargo, producen en su conjunto un efecto de gran novedad, precisamente por el modo cómo están distribuídos y tratados en la composición. Los planos de ésta hállanse distribuídos de un modo grandioso y todo está tratado enfáticamente.

El frente, dividido en tres tableros encuadrados por la parte inferior y laterales con armadura de marco ensamblada a inglete, mostrando en su disposición una lógica constructiva perfecta, dando a los costados el valor de simples montantes y reservando para la base mayor dimensión; decorándolo a escala más reducida que en el centro, pero perfectamente relacionada en sus proporciones con los temas decorativos del centro; estableciendo así la debida separación entre contenido y continente. Este efecto se completa con el resalte que tiene dicho marco, con relación al plano del tablero central. En este mismo tablero central, con el emblema del Sacramento y tema de las rosetas, se consigue un decorado de gran sobriedad, pareciendo hecho de intento para realzar de un modo solemne todo el valor de dicho emblema.

Ese mueble es otro de los ejemplos de arte popular lleno de enseñanzas para un arte suntuoso y sabio.

Propiedad particular, en Palma de Mallorca. - Fot. del Arx. Mas.

60

XLIV

61. XVII century chest used by the provincial middle class. Its simple composition is formed by lozenges inscribed within rectangles and the carver filled the entire surface with decoration, varying the dimensions of the designs on each band to fit the available space. At the center the lozenges alternate with bands of tiny leaves that soften the harsh lines of the geometric forms; they also accentuate the massiveness of the chest. National Museum of Decorative Arts, Madrid.

LÁMINA XLIV, *fig. 61.*ª - Arcón del siglo XVII; mueble al servicio de la clase media popular. Su composición es muy simple, formada por rombos inscritos en espacios rectangulares siguiendo su directriz la mayor dimensión decorable y alterando sus dimensiones según los múltiplos posibles en cada faja. En el centro, los rombos se alternan con fajas de menudas hojas que hacen cambiar el aspecto de sequedad lineal que domina en las formas geométricas, y sirven también para acentuar la grandiosidad aparente de éstas. El conjunto es de gran sencillez.

Museo Nacional de Artes Industriales, de Madrid. - Fot. de R. Doménech.

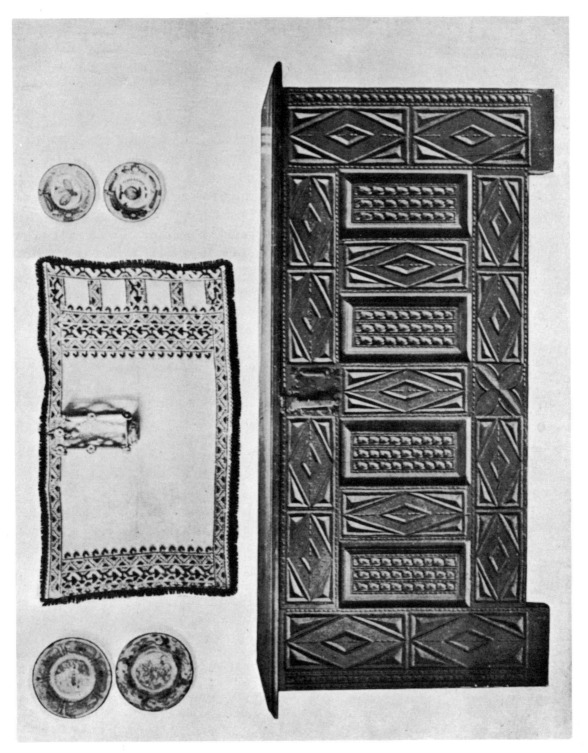

XLV

62. XVII century three-storied cabinet with marked disproportion between its height and width. It is made in the style of a monk's *vargueño,* with the addition of an upper story. The front is decorated with fine inlay, but the ironwork on the central body has no relation to this kind of decoration. The heaviness of the crosspieces on the upper story is out of proportion to the slenderness of the balusters, but despite these defects the whole is not in bad taste. Private Collection.

LÁMINA XLV, *fig. 62.*ª - Armario del siglo XVII, compuesto de tres cuerpos. Marcada desproporción entre su altura y ancho; carácter de vargueño frailero, con el aditamento del cuerpo superior. Decoración en fina taracea; los herrajes del cuerpo central nada tienen que ver con esa decoración.

En el cuerpo superior, pesan los peinazos por la desproporción que tienen con la delgadez de las columnillas. A pesar de esos defectos, tiene un conjunto nada vulgar.

Col. particular. - Fot. de J. Roig.

62

XLVI

63. Two-storied cabinet with geometric boxwood inlay. Definitely Spanish, it is typical of some provincial work from the second half of the XVII century through the XVIII. It is very similar to the one shown in the previous picture, but lacks the central story and the pediment. The size of the crosspieces and balusters on the upper story of this cabinet are in better proportion. Private Collection.

LÁMINA XLVI, *fig. 63.*ª - Armario de dos cuerpos, con taraceas de boj formando decoraciones geométricas. Es un mueble francamente español, de la segunda mitad del siglo XVII y todo el XVIII, muy típico en algunas regiones de España.

Tiene gran semejanza con el reproducido en la lámina anterior, faltándole el cuerpo central y el remate en forma de frontón. El volumen de peinazos y balaustres del cuerpo superior están mejor proporcionados en este armario.

Propiedad particular. -

XLVII

64. XVI century Spanish wardrobe used in the sacristy of a church, decorated with gilded carving and polychrome designs. An extraordinary example because of its rarity and elegance. Private Collection, Madrid.

LÁMINA XLVII, *fig. 64.ª* - Armario español del siglo XVI, de servicio en la sacristía de algún templo. Decoración hecha con tallas y policromía con oro. Tipo extraordinario por su rareza y elegancia.

De propiedad particular. - Madrid.

64

XLVIII

65. Spanish XVII century walnut table with carved drawers. The drawer fronts are decorated in the *mudéjar* tradition. This piece of furniture is similar to the table in Figure 66, and the same comments apply. The differences between the front and back legs is a result of their rectilinear shape, which gives them a decorative quality related to the profusion of decorative elements on the upper part. National Museum of Decorative Arts, Madrid.

LÁMINA XLVIII, *fig. 65.ª* - Mesa de nogal con cajonería tallada; tipo español del siglo XVII. Las unidades que decoran los frentes de la cajonería son de tradición mudéjar.

Puede repetirse en el estudio de este mueble todo lo que se expone en las notas relativas a la lámina XLIX. Las ligeras variantes en los pies son consecuencia del sistema rectilíneo adoptado en los mismos, aligerando sus planos y dándoles un valor decorativo que esté relacionado con la profusión de elementos de embellecimiento que hay en la parte superior.

Museo Nacional de Artes Industriales, de Madrid.—Fot. de R. Doménech.

XLIX

66. Spanish XVII century walnut table with carved drawers. The motifs on the drawers are typical of provincial art in the old Romanesque tradition. A striking pecularity is the way that the spaces beside the drawers are defined: the two above the legs are smooth and slightly decorated, but the two central ones project as fluted brackets, creating a strikingly original effect. The geometric rosettes on the drawers are a simple decoration and the change of motif at the center is well calculated to avoid any possible monotony. The heavy, ring-shaped drawer pulls harmonize well with the robust appearance of the piece. National Museum of Decorative Arts, Madrid.

LÁMINA XLIX, *fig. 66.*ª - Mesa de nogal con cajonería tallada. Tipo español del siglo XVII. Las unidades que decoran la cajonería son típicamente populares, de antigua tradición romanizante.

Son rasgos muy salientes los que determinan los espacios divisorios de la cajonería, siendo planos y ligeramente decorados en la parte superior de los pies de este mueble y en resaltos a modo de modillones estriados en los otros dos centrales. El efecto es de gran originalidad. Las rosetas geométricas de los cajones dan por resultado una decoración severa y el cambio de motivo en el centro está bien calculado para evitar una posible monotonía. Los tiradores, en forma de gruesas anillas, se hermanan muy bien con el aspecto robusto de todo el mueble.

Museo Nacional de Artes Industriales, de Madrid.—Fot. de R. Doménech.

L

67. Table with carved drawer fronts, from the first third of the XVIII century. National Museum of Decorative Arts, Madrid.

LÁMINA L, *fig. 67.ª* - Mesa con cajonería de frentes tallados. Tipo español del primer tercio del siglo XVIII.

Museo Nacional de Artes Industriales, de Madrid.—Fot. de R. Doménech.

LI

68. Table with lyre supports and beautiful iron braces with scrolls ending in fleurons. The fronts of the drawers are carved in low relief. Second half of the XVII century. Private Collection.

LÁMINA LI, *fig. 68.*ª - Mesa con pies de lira y hermosos fiadores de hierro, cuyas volutas rematan en florones. Los frentes de la cajonería están decorados con tallas en bajo relieve. Tipo de la segunda mitad del siglo XVII.

De colección particular.—Fot. del Arx. Mas.

68

LII

69. Walnut table decorated with carving in low relief. XVII century Spanish type, in a transitional style between provincial and urban. The robust decoration harmonizes with the sturdy, rather massive shape of the piece. Some of the decorations show heaviness; for example, the terminal spirals of the rosettes do not combine well with the radiating centers. Because of its proportions, this table is very different from those reproduced in the previous pictures. National Museum of Decorative Arts, Madrid.

LÁMINA LII, *fig. 69.*ª - Mesa de nogal decorada con tallas en bajo relieve. Tipo español del siglo XVII, de transición del arte popular al suntuoso.

La decoración robusta de ese mueble está en consonancia con su forma recia, un tanto pesada, que le da el volumen de sus masas constructivas. Algunas soluciones decorativas indican algo de torpeza, como, por ejemplo, en las espiras terminales de los florones, que no unen bien con los centros radiados de los mismos.

Esa mesa, por sus proporciones ofrece una gran diferencia con las reproducidas en las láminas anteriores.

Museo Nacional de Artes Industriales, de Madrid.—Fot. de R. Doménech.

LIII

70. Walnut bench with back carved in low relief, from the Spanish Renaissance, late XVI century. This bench lacks the grace and elegance of the one reproduced in the next figure, but has more pretensions to being an important work of art. The aristocratic decoration on the back is in perfect harmony with the heraldic shield at the center. National Museum of Decorative Arts, Madrid.

LÁMINA LIII, *fig. 70.*ª - Banco de nogal con respaldo tallado en bajo relieve. Trabajo español de fines del siglo XVI, en estilo Renacimiento.

Sin la claridad y elegancia de composición del banco que se reproduce en la lámina LIV, pero con más pretensiones de obra de arte importante. Tiene un marcado caracter señorial el conjunto decorativo del respaldo, en perfecta consonancia con el escudo nobiliario del centro.

Museo Nacional de Artes Industriales, de Madrid.—Fot. de R. Doménech.

70

LIV

71. XVII century bench with a pierced iron plaque at the center of the back. All of the charm of this piece is concentrated on the back; the very elegant composition is easily understood because of the excellent balance between the decorative masses and the background. Private Collection.

LÁMINA LIV, *fig. 71.*ª - Banco del siglo XVII. El centro del respaldo es de plancha sobrecalada.

Todo el encanto de este mueble está concentrado en el respaldo cuya composición elegantísima resulta sumamente inteligible, por la compensación muy justa de las masas decorativas con el fondo.

De propiedad particular.—Fot. de J. Roig.

LV

72. XVII century bench. The construction of this bench resembles some chairs of the same period, especially the one reproduced in Figure 6. The decoration is simple inlay. Because of the importance of the silhouette and the distribution of the masses, the bench is elegant and restrained. Private Collection.

LÁMINA LV, *fig. 72.*ª - Banco del siglo XVII. La composición de este banco recuerda la de aquellas sillas de la misma época, publicadas en las primeras láminas y especialmente la reproducida en la figura 6.ª. La decoración es muy sencilla, hecha con taraceas; el conjunto, por el valor de la silueta y distribución de las masas, resulta elegante y severo.

Col. particular.—Fot. de J. Roig.

LVI

73. Bed with turned posts and an arcaded headboard carved in low relief. This XVII century style persisted in Spain through the first third of the XVIII century.

Lámina LVI, *fig. 73.ª* - Cama cabecera de arquería, talla en bajo relieve y pies torneados. Tipo del siglo XVII, cuya forma perdura en España durante el primer tercio del siglo XVIII.

Fot. del Arx. Mas.

73

LVII

74. Bronze or copper brazier with embossed edge and handles. The stand is made of two rings joined by turned legs, and the upper ring is decorated with inlay. The piece is typical of the late XVII century. Its beauty is the result of the successful use of its materials: embossed metal and wood with inlaid decoration on the upper ring and balusters, all in an excellent arrangement. Separately, these elements are of secondary worth. Collection of the Marquis de la Cénia, Palma de Mallorca.

LÁMINA LVII, *fig. 74.*ª - Brasero de bronce o cobre con el alero o borde y las asas relevadas. Caja de doble anillo unidos por pies torneados. El anillo superior decorado con taraceas. Ejemplar típico de fines del siglo XVII. La belleza de este mueble está conseguida por el acertado empleo de sus elementos materiales, el metal relevado con el brillo de sus aristas, la madera con su decoración de taraceas en el anillo superior y los balaustres, todo en una excelente agrupación. Separadamente, esos elementos son de un valor secundario.

Col. del Excmo. Sr. Marqués de la Cenia, Palma de Mallorca.—Fot. del Arx. Mas.

LVIII

75-77. Carved decorations from old Spanish furniture. The National Museum of Decorative Arts at Madrid has assembled a large series of old Spanish carving patterns used for furniture decoration, and some of them are illustrated here, reproduced in wood.

All furniture should be built to fulfill a definite purpose. From this purpose and from the properties of wood, furniture acquires a shape with special meaning for each period and country—a shape much more decisive than most of the public and many cabinetmakers believe. Such furniture, even if decorated with carved designs copied from older pieces, can be handsome, Spanish and contemporary.

The adaptation of these decorative components is not easy. The cabinetmaker or designer must know what each type of carved decoration, such as borders and rosettes, can accomplish by its volume, character, and play of light, and he must harmonize them with the style of the piece and the part to be decorated. As the furniture in this book illustrates, great beauty is often achieved through the skillful use of common themes. The craftsman must take care to use appropriate borders; the border that forms a proper frame for elements whose carving is sharp and deep would not harmonize with elements whose carving is round and smooth. Confusion results if the effect of their shadings blends with that of the borders, because both surfaces have the same value. Rosettes too can be repeated or alternated to form borders with varying aesthetic effect. National Museum of Decorative Arts, Madrid.

LÁMINAS LVIII A LX - Decoraciones en tallas de muebles antiguos españoles.

El Museo Nacional de Artes Industriales, de Madrid, está formando grandes series de antiguas tallas españolas ejecutadas en la decoración de muebles, como viene realizando lo mismo con unidades decorativas de bordados y de cerámica nacional. Las tallas se reproducen en madera con toda fidelidad, y forman un gran *corpus* de documentación para el estudio de ese aspecto del mobiliario español antiguo y para un posible trabajo en el moderno.

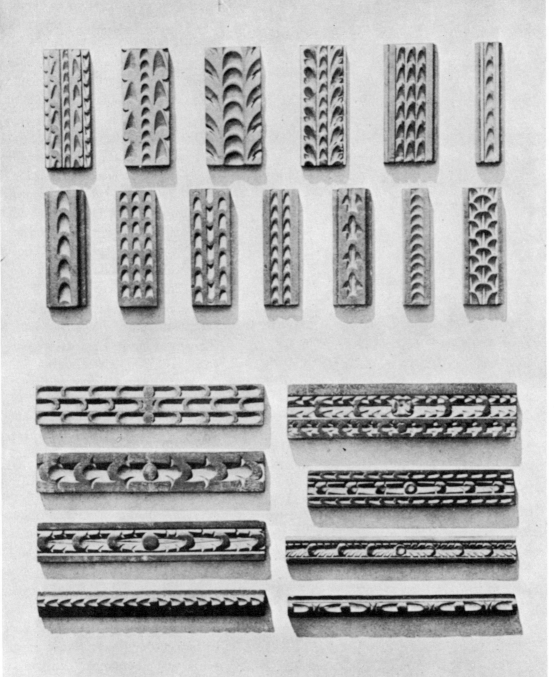

LIX

Todo mueble, respondiendo a una necesidad de la vida, debe construirse de modo que cumpla bien esa necesidad. De ese principio y de las condiciones materiales de la madera, nace la forma del mueble y adquiere así un valor personal de tiempo y país, mucho más enérgico de lo que pueda creer gran parte del público y no pocos ebanistas.

El mueble así construído puede embellecerse con tallas y sin que sus unidades sean originales, sino copiadas, por la buena distribución de ellas y la acertada elección de las mismas puede llegar a formar un hermoso mueble, español y contemporáneo.

El empleo de esos elementos decorativos no es fácil. Es preciso saber lo que vale cada tipo de decoración tallada (fajas, rosetones, etc.), por su masa, por su carácter y por el juego de luces, para armonizarlos con las formas del mueble, con la parte de éste que decoren, y por último, para que entre unos temas decorativos de tallas y otros haya una perfecta coesión.

Con frecuencia ·hemos visto, al analizar los muebles publicados en esta obra, cómo se conseguía una gran belleza con temas de uso corriente, gracias a un acertado empleo de los mismos.

En el uso de las fajas hay que tomar en cuenta lo siguiente: suelen encuadrar plementos cuya talla, más o menos profusa, puede ofrecer planos de aristas vivas y enérgicas, o por el contrario, redondeadas y suaves en los efectos de claro obscuro. Si el valor total de esos obscuros llega a confundirse con el de las fajas de encuadratura, el resultado es nulo por la confusión que se origina, pues todo tendrá el mismo valor. Lo mismo puede decirse de los rosetones; con éstos pueden componerse fajas, empleando un ritmo de repetición o de alternancia, consiguiendo efectos de caracter estético muy variados.

Museo Nacional de Artes Industriales de Madrid.—Fot. de R. Doménech.

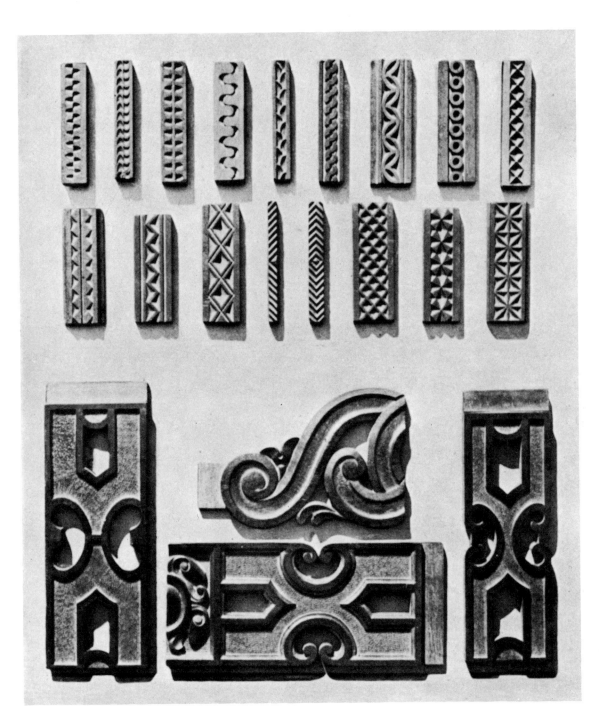

LX

For
my son Keenan who, like the
sea, is an endless source of
inspiration and inner beauty.

WGB

COLORS
OF THE
SEA

PHOTOGRAPHY BY W. GREGORY BROWN ■ TEXT BY OWEN ANDREWS

ELLIOTT & CLARK PUBLISHING, INC. ■ ■ WASHINGTON, D.C. ■ ■

Acknowledgments

A very special thanks to Steve Frelich, the man who granted my wishes, and to Captain Greg Lawlor and the crew of the *Mollie Dean*, the world's finest memory makers.   —W. Gregory Brown

(PAGE 1) NAMENALALA BARRIER REEF, FIJI.

(PAGE 2-3) NORTH ASTROLABE REEF, FIJI

(PAGE 7) ARC-EYED HAWKFISH,

Paracirrhites arcuatus, WAKAYA PASSAGE, FIJI.

Designed by Deborah Frelich, Image Hunter Company

Edited by Carolyn M. Clark

Text by Owen Andrews

Production by Sandi Hettler

ISBN 1-880216-02-7

Printed in Singapore by Tien Wah Press

5   4   3   2   1   1999   1998

1997 1996 1995 1994 1993 1992

Library of Congress Cataloging-In-Publication Data

Brown, W. Gregory (William Gregory), 1954-
   Colors of the sea/photography by
W. Gregory Brown: text by Owen Andrews.
      p. cm.
   Includes index.
   ISBN 1-880216-02-7
   1. Coral reef ecology. 2. Coral reef ecology—
Pictorial works. 3. Underwater photography.
I. Andrews. Owen. 1957- . II. Title.
QH541.5.C7B76   1992
574.5'26367—dc20
91-34697
   CIP

TABLE OF CONTENTS

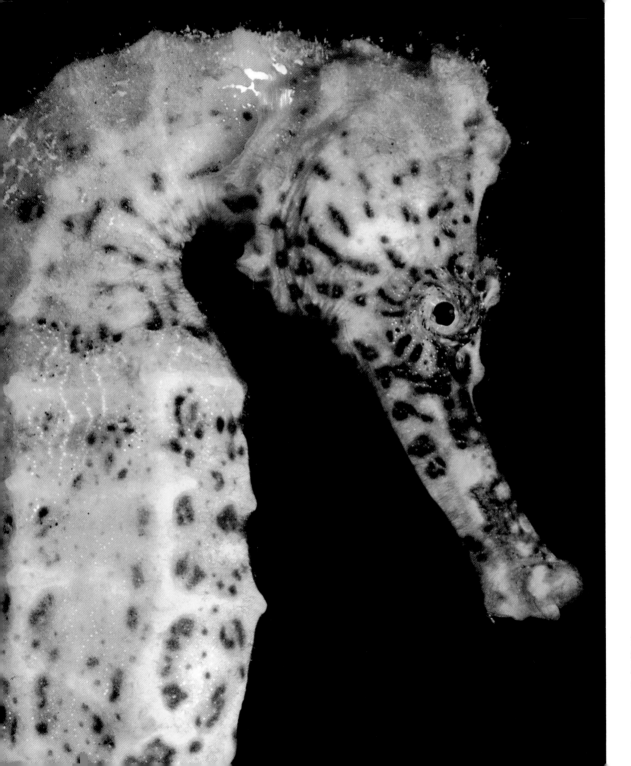

YELLOW
SEAHORSE,
*Hippocampus
reidi.*

If coral reefs flourished in any pond or stream or bay, would our imaginations be as delighted by their abundant life? As it is, reefs are often far from home, in places we equate with Eden or at least a winter vacation, places where the water isn't icy, murky, and green, but warm and astonishingly clear.

Not only are many of the world's great reefs remote, but to most human societies, these ancient ecosystems, with a history reaching back over 400 million years, are truly new, glimpsed only in the last few decades. The lucky few who have always lived in the major coral-growing zones have known about them all along: hundreds of years ago, in Polynesia, spearfishermen wore tortoiseshell goggles to see better as they dove; in Central America, the Mayans maintained fishing outposts near Belize's barrier reef. And in the Mediterranean, the search for sponges and precious red coral created a 2,000-year-old tradition of free diving at depths as great as 200 feet.

We know that early Polynesians understood reef life well enough to lay down hunting guidelines that discouraged overfishing. But until scuba gear and underwater cameras came along, prolonged observation and detailed, accurate recording of the reef's mind-boggling complexity were impossible. These devices have spawned a flood of knowledge which is only the introduction to a true understanding of the living coral reef.

In these pages, photographer and marine biologist W. Gregory Brown's images are a welcome reminder that the more we see and the more we learn, the more certain it is that divers can visit a coral reef every day and never grow tired of what they find.

REEF
BUILDERS

ROCK
ISLANDS,
PALAU.

Measured in square miles, coral reefs cover a far smaller part of the planet than other significant ecosystems such as grasslands, forests, and deserts. Square foot for square foot, however, a coral reef is matched only by the tropical rain forest in its abundance of species. And perhaps no place on earth can match a reef, inch for inch, for the visual intensity of its brilliantly colored mobile inhabitants and the infinitely varied shapes and forms of its stationary ones.

This alone sets the world's reefs apart from all other habitats. From a biological perspective, the reef differs in an even more basic way. It is the only one whose structure is provided by the growth of animals rather than plants: millions of tiny polyps, stationary relatives of jellyfish and sea anemones, live in colonies connected and defended by a framework of limestone.

This uniquely constructed ecosystem is also one of the planet's oldest. Geologists have found evidence of reefs that existed in the tropics during the Ordovician Period, over 400 million years ago. The species which built those reefs vanished during a period of mass extinctions 200 million years later. About 180 million years ago, a new family of hard corals appeared, the *Scleractinia,* and from them descend the reef-building species that exist today.

Despite their antiquity, hard or reef-building corals do not appear to have adapted to colder climates any better than their ancestors did. They are still found, for the most part, near the equator, between the tropics of Cancer and Capricorn, in the shallows of the planet's warmest ocean waters. A curious partnership limits *Scleractinia* to the clearest areas of the tropical ocean.

Animals though they be, hard-coral polyps are home to a throng of one-celled plants, the algae zooxanthellae. Through an amazingly thrifty biochemical partnership with zooxanthellae, hard corals grow in waters that are virtual marine deserts. For it turns out that the glassy clarity of tropical seas so prized by vacationers is proof of a distinct shortage of plankton, the tiny organisms which form the base of the marine food chain.

Coral and zooxanthellae make the most of the available nutrients by means of a continuous exchange of by-products. Digesting plankton, each coral polyp creates phosphate and nitrogen wastes, excellent nutrients for plants. As they absorb and process these wastes, the algae produce sugars—food for the corals—which are digested in their turn. In addition, the presence of zooxanthellae causes tropical hard corals to amass their limestone structures far more quickly than the few hard-coral species which do not house these algae.

Zooxanthellae require two things of their coral hosts. As plants, they need enough sunlight to carry on photosynthesis, which limits them to within 300 feet of the surface and ideally to depths between 20 and 60 feet. As partners in a specific sequence of biochemical transactions, they require steady temperatures, roughly between 70° and 90° Fahrenheit.

With these conditions in mind, it seems reasonable to expect that coral reefs would be evenly spread around most continental and island shores in the tropics. In fact, the tropical western coasts of the Americas, Australia, and Africa have far fewer coral reefs than their eastern counterparts.

The cause lies far to the south, in the immense quantities of cold water surrounding Antarctica. From these frigid seas, ocean currents sweep northward past the western coasts of the nearest continents. These currents are so strong that even off western Central America north of the equator, reef-building corals are scarce, while a few hundred miles due east, off the coast of Belize in the Caribbean, the western hemisphere's largest barrier reef stretches for 150 miles.

Divers who visit reefs in both Indo-Pacific and Caribbean waters immediately see a difference between them. Sponges commonly appear throughout the Caribbean, while *Dendronephthya* are the hallmark in the Indo-Pacific. Moreover, the Indo-Pacific contains more hard-coral species than the Caribbean—perhaps 400 compared to the Caribbean's 50.

Again, glacial ice may be the cause. During the ice ages, the cooling effect of the glaciers that covered half of North America was enough to kill off many of the hard-coral species in the Caribbean basin—species the Caribbean had probably shared with the Indo-Pacific since before the shifting of the continents divided the oceans.

Today's descriptions of the forms reefs take as they grow are based on the speculations of Charles Darwin, who chanced to make observations at a coral reef in the Indian Ocean 150 years ago. Darwin devised a theory to describe a typical volcanic island which develops a surrounding reef. In the beginning, reef-building corals grow on the island's underwater slopes not far from shore, forming a fringing reef.

Over time, geological factors may cause the island to subside into the water. Or the sea level may rise, as it did when the glaciers of the last ice age melted. Then, as the expanse of water between the reef and the shore grows larger, a lagoon develops. As long as the sea does not rise too quickly and the corals keep growing to the necessary distance from the surface, the fringing reef is gradually transformed into a ring, or barrier reef, around the sinking island.

Eventually, the volcanic landmass may simply disappear under water, drowned by rising seas, or hastened in its descent by the sheer weight of water in its surrounding lagoon. Then the barrier reef becomes an atoll, a ring of coral around a blue lagoon. Most true atolls are found in the remote island chains of the South Pacific.

If the landmass is a continent rather than an island, the barrier is the reef's final form—as in the case of the Great Barrier Reef off Australia's northeast coast. The largest coral assemblage in the world, claiming over 200 coral species and countless other life forms, it is a place where students of reef denizens from gobies to nudibranchs continue to discover new species. ■ ■

TWIXT REEF,
BONAIRE,
NETHERLANDS
ANTILLES.
*Beautiful tube
sponges and vase
sponges are
trademarks of
reefs in the
Caribbean Sea.*

JACKSON REEF,
RED SEA.
Dendronephthya
*soft corals,
unique to the
Indo-Pacific,
flourish in the
currents and clear
waters of the
Red Sea.*

PEPPERMINT
GOBY,
Coryphopterus
lipernes,
NETHERLANDS
ANTILLES.

When we think of carnivorous animals, we think of lions, bears, and crocodiles—powerful creatures which fear nothing in their territories. Or we think of less fearsome, equally fast-moving animals such as hawks or house cats, or insect-eating birds, bats, and geckos.

All of these carnivores share one trait. When the chance of a meal presents itself, they move decisively to claim it. On land, few creature-eating creatures survive just by sitting around with their mouths open.

The underwater world also has its share of fast-moving predators, some as large as sharks and some as small and fragile-looking as the longnose hawkfish. Many underwater carnivores, however, are sessile creatures, gathering their prey from a fixed position. They really do survive by opening their mouths and waiting for something to fall in. Many of the coelenterates (from the Greek for "stomach"), including soft and hard corals and sea anemones, are among the stationary feeders.

Plankton, the drifting mass of microscopic species at the base of the marine food chain, is the main food for which most of these creatures wait. Looked at closely, plankton turns out to be a diverse crowd of minute relatives of larger marine species, too small to swim effectively in the current.

Most nutritious among plankton are the crustaceans: waterfleas, isopods, copepods, and many others. Where these are plentiful, all marine life abounds. Equally important are the larval stages of many larger marine species, including crustaceans such as shrimps, lobsters, and crabs; coelenterates such as jellyfish, medusae, and corals themselves; sponges; mollusks; and the eggs of many fish species.

The look of the coral-reef community, the amazing variety of shapes and forms which a diver swims through, follows from the corals' myriad strategies for trapping floating particles of food. Among the hard corals, which must also ensure that sunlight reaches their zooxanthellae, the need for the colony to present as much surface area as possible to sunlight and currents produces every shape from a squat boulder to a cluster of tall pillars.

The names for these corals suggest the possibilities. The spherical mass of brain-coral colonies, and the sinuous, tightly enfolded rows along which their polyps lie, have the look of the cerebellum. Table-coral colonies swell out over a central stem, a shape that allows them to shade out competing neighbors. Elkhorn coral, a signature species on many Caribbean reefs, adopts a branching structure to obtain exposure to sunlight and plankton near the surface. The lettuce corals of the Indo-Pacific are among the many species which can produce wide, flattish discs with spiraling patterns—another excellent way to receive a lot of sunlight.

Among soft corals, gorgonians spread their branches in a broad, flat fan at right angles to the current. The alcyonarians, which grow in both warm and cold waters, duplicate the strategy of a tree, putting out branches from a substantial trunk.

Many of these corals feed primarily at night. As evening comes, their polyps inflate with seawater, and their tentacles reach out. To draw in plankton, they rely on the movements of their tentacles, the slight draw created by the intake of water into the stomach cavity as they continuously pump water through their bodies, and also on the action of a type of stinging cell found only among corals and their cnidarian relatives.

Of the reef's other stationary plankton feeders found in the Caribbean and the Indo-Pacific, the feather stars, or crinoids, comprise an especially curious-looking group. These ancient relatives of sea stars use their thin, leglike cirri to walk up to small prominences on the reef, uncurl their plumelike arms, and extend them into the current. As plankton gets caught in the bristles of each arm, rows of cilia push them down toward grooves in the bristles' spines. This in turn leads to a groove, also lined with cilia, running straight down each arm of the crinoid to the central stomach.

Plankton is not only the diet of stationary creatures. Fishes as small as *Anthias* basslets and as large as manta rays also depend on it. *Anthias* snap up individual plankton much as birds or bats nab mosquitos in midair. The manta ray, on the other hand, sometimes swims near the reef with its mouth agape, sweeping in all the plankton it encounters—a feeding technique that works well enough for the largest of the rays to reach weights as great as a ton.

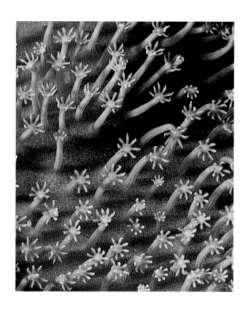

Sarcophyton trocheliophorum, NORTH ASTROLABE REEF, FIJI. *Sarcophyton feeds during the day, a rarity among corals. The colony forms a supple, curving dish.*

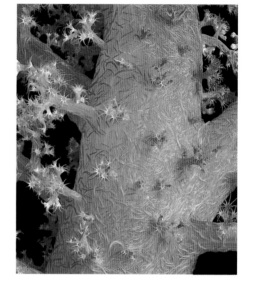

Dendronephthya klunzingeri, RAS UMM SID, RED SEA. *Dendronephthya feed at night; the entire soft-coral colony expands with seawater as branches reach into the current.*

MUSHROOM CORAL, *Fungia fungites,* TRUK LAGOON. *This coral is about to release thousands of gametes, most of which will be eaten as plankton. One or two may be fertilized and begin a new colony.*

GORGONIAN, *Melithaea squamata,* PALAU. *Gorgonians are made of a fingernail-like protein substance that can withstand strong currents.*

NAMENALALA ISLAND, FIJI. *Several gorgonian species and an unusual white crinoid flourish around this tunnel opening.*

SCARLET SEA WHIPS, *Ellisella sp.*, TURTLE COVE, PALAU. *Each specimen of this soft coral may have as many as 30 to 40 whips, two-foot-long scarlet strands covered with white polyps.*

Dendronephthya klunzingeri, GREAT WHITE WALL, FIJI. *Spicules, deposits of calcium carbonate, stiffen* Dendronephthya's *soft, fleshy structure.*

GARDEN EEL, *Taenioconger hassi*, PALAU. *Garden eels are daylight feeders, prospecting for plankton from burrows into which they instantly retreat at the slightest danger.*

MANTA RAY *Manta birostris* WAILANGILALA ATOLL, FIJI *These spectacular swimmers frequently feed around reef passages where currents are strong and plankton abundant.*

ROUGH
FILE SHELL, *Lima
scabra*, CAYMAN
BRAC. *On rare
forays into the
open from its
crevice on the
reef, the rough
file shell moves
around on jets of
water by shutting
and opening its
valves.*

FAIRY BASSLET, *Gramma loreto,* BONAIRE. *Fairy basslets forage for plankton on Caribbean reef slopes, hovering at depths of 30 to 60 feet.*

(INSET) CRINOID, ORDER COMATULIDA, TURTLE COVE, PALAU. *A crinoid's feathery arms are easily broken. But like a sea star, it will grow a new limb in the old one's place.*

ORANGE-CUP
CORAL,
Tubastraea aurea,
BONAIRE. *Lacking
zooxanthellae,
orange-cup corals
do not need light;
they are found in
small colonies
under ledges and
in caves.*

LYRETAIL
CORALFISH,
*Anthias
squamipinnis*,
USBOURNE
PASSAGE,
ASTROLABE REEF.
*Almost every fish
of this species is
born female. As
older males die,
dominant females
change sex and
replace them as
the heads of
female harems.*

EMBER
PARROTFISH,
*Scarus
rubroviolaceus,*
ASTROLABE REEF.

CORAL

FEEDERS

Solidly encased in their limestone secretions, living corals would seem to be safe from the appetites of other reef dwellers. But coral is too rich and reliable a source of protein and algae to be left alone. Many types of creatures, from fishes to sponges and sea stars, have found ways to subsist partially or entirely on coral.

A fish needs a special kind of mouth to get at coral, and among the coral-grazing species, two basic types can be seen: algae-scrapers and polyp-nippers. Best known among the algae-scrapers are the parrotfishes. Swimming along the reef, divers may observe their handiwork, an irregular pattern of scratches on algae-covered portions. But parrotfishes don't limit themselves to scraping surfaces. With their strong jaws and fused rows of teeth, they bite off knobs and chunks of coral, then pass them back to a second set of teeth in the pharynx, where they are broken down.

A parrotfish doesn't actually digest the limestone portion of its meal. After its digestive tract has extracted all the nutritious algae it can from the stony mass, the rest is passed out of the parrotfish in a fine spray of coral sand.

As a parrotfish must eat a lot of coral stone to obtain adequate nutrition, the production of sand goes on all day. Some researchers have estimated that a parrotfish unloads as much as five pounds of coral sand every day.

Mouth shapes among the coral-nipping fishes indicate feeding habits. The longnose butterflyfish and the longnose filefish, with oral equipment that resembles a pair of needle-nosed pliers, are perfectly outfitted to poke into coral cups and pull out polyps. Other fishes with protruding mouths sometimes reach into crannies along the reef and extract the creatures that hide in these protected places.

Butterflyfishes are by far the most conspicuous coral grazers; divers are delighted by their brilliant coloring and delicate movements as they browse through the sunny shallows of the reef. Many butterflyfishes form long-term pair bonds and patrol a specific portion of the reef. They can be elusive, maintaining a precise distance between themselves and divers and disappearing into a crevice at the first hint of danger. Grazing so close to the reef has one clear defensive advantage: shelter is nearby in one of the reef's countless nooks and crannies.

Those nooks and crannies are an important reason for the abundance of life on the reef. As corals and the other limestone-depositing creatures grow, their shapes fit together in ways that create caves, tunnels, crevices, overhangs, shelves, and burrows where other creatures seek a permanent foothold or a temporary shelter.

Some creatures go further, improving their defenses by digging into the coral structure. Microscopic sponges, *Cliona*, use chemicals and digging components to honeycomb living and dead corals. Date mussels and many other mollusks and snails bore larger holes in coral, while some bivalves and worms create snug pockets from which they can extend their feeding mechanisms. When they die and their remains are scavenged from their homes, other creatures move in. Sometimes a section of the reef will have been so thoroughly drilled that it collapses. It's estimated that living organisms are responsible for fully half of all reef erosion.

Crawling along the reef or subtly posed against other brightly colored reef organisms, the nudibranchs must be ranked among the most visually arresting of reef-dwelling algae and coral feeders. Nudibranchs are small snails without shells, half an inch to three inches long, and their name means "naked gill" in Greek. The Aeolids are the coral eaters; other nudibranch families eat a wide variety of foods available on the reef. They digest their food not with a stomach but with a radula, a kind of ribbon set with a variety of microscopic teeth.

Despite their soft, fleshy bodies, nudibranchs are of little interest to predators, as they reportedly have an extremely unpleasant flavor. Moreover, the coral-eating nudibranchs have evolved a fascinating defense as they consume polyps.

Along the surfaces of coral polyps' tentacles, numerous stinging cells are lodged between the other tissues. Each of these tiny cells is loaded with a harpoonlike thread, covered with barbs, which shoots out on contact toward whatever triggers it. Some nudibranchs, however, have found a way not only to ingest these cells, but to direct them to small protuberances on their backs, where they are recycled as stinging cells for their new hosts. Few examples could illustrate more concisely the amazing orchestration of resources on the reef.

LONGNOSE FILEFISH, *Oxymonocanthus longirostris*, NAVATU ATOLL, FIJI. *Groves of staghorn coral attract longnose filefish, which bite off polyps with their elongated mouths.*

QUEEN ANGELFISH, *Holocanthus ciliarus*, BONAIRE. *The colors of these foot-long fish shift with movement, creating a shimmering blend of greens, yellows, and blues.*

MASKED BUTTER-FLYFISH, *Chaetodon semilarvatus*, RAS MOHAMMED, RED SEA. *The masked butterflyfish, a Red Sea species, is usually found in mated pairs or small schools.*

OCELLATED
NUDIBRANCH,
Phyllidia ocellata,
NORTH
ASTROLABE
LAGOON.
*Like almost all
sea slugs, the
ocellated nudi-
branch is active
primarily at night,
when it feeds
on sponges.*

CHROMODORID,
Chromodoris sp.,
PALAU. *Found at
depths of 30 to
90 feet, this nudi-
branch moves
with an
unmistakable
fluttering and
flaring of its
purple-edged
mantle.*

RUFFLE-BACKED SLUG, *Tridachia crispata*, BONAIRE. *In shallow Caribbean waters, the ruffle-backed slug punctures cells of algae with its microscopic teeth and sucks out the liquid.*

FLAMINGO-TONGUE, *Cyphoma gibbosum*, GRAND CAYMAN ISLAND. *A relative of cowries, flamingo-tongues live on sea fans, leaving a dark trail where their radulae have scraped off polyps and mucus.*

41

SEA STAR,
Fromia monilis,
PALAU. *Sea stars
move by stretching
an arm, gripping
something solid,
and pulling
the other arms
forward.*

EYESTALKS OF
SPIDER CONCH,
Lambis crocata,
DUFF REEF, FIJI.
*Known for their
unusual shells
lined with a
handful of spidery
prongs, spider
conchs feed on
algae and plant
detritus.*

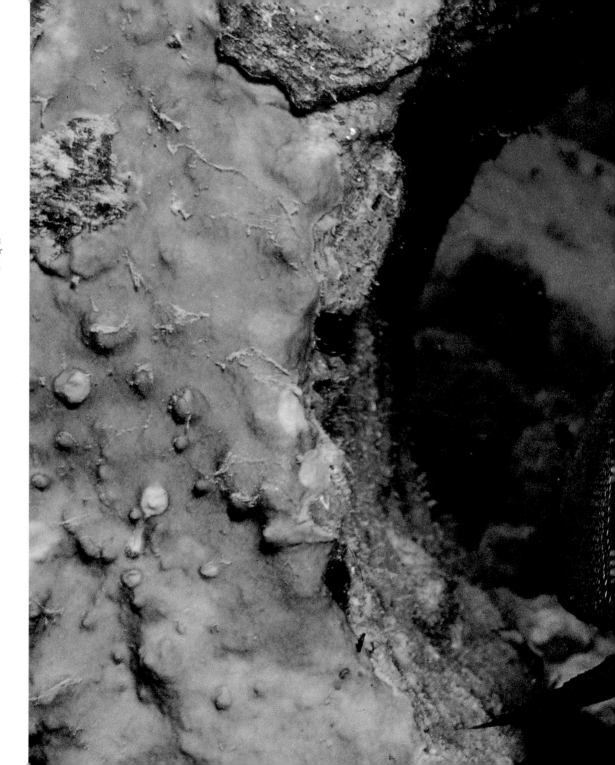

FRENCH ANGELFISH, *Pomacanthus paru*, WRECK OF THE *RHONE*, BRITISH VIRGIN ISLANDS. *Deftly turning and darting, angelfish keep close to reef structures, where they feed on soft corals and other sessile species.*

Hunters

One of the rarest things for a diver to see on the reef is a fish in the act of eating another fish. It happens all the time, of course. But it happens very quickly. What divers are likely to see, if they see anything at all, is one fish swimming where two fish swam before.

To Greg Brown, the sight was so out of the ordinary that when he saw another underwater photographer's image of a lizardfish biting down on a false cleaner blenny a couple of years ago, he assumed the shot had been set up somehow. In ten years of diving and photographing, he had never seen a fish in another's mouth. Ten days later, he was diving in Fiji and happened to see similar species in the same situation (pages 52-3).

A hunting fish needs to move quickly, because the fishes it preys on, by and large, can accelerate with great rapidity. Some fish, it has been estimated, go from a standstill to full speed in about 1/20th of a second. This helps explain why predators and prey are sometimes seen swimming in each other's vicinity. As long as the distance between them is adequate, the predator can't close the gap before its target reaches safety.

Fishes, like all other animals, must always favor behavior that minimizes effort and maximizes return. Therefore, most predatory fishes conceal themselves from their prey in a number of different ways, saving their energy for a quick lunge.

Among the true artists of concealment on the reef are the stonefishes and scorpionfishes. These creatures' bodies are covered with ugly protuberances, algaelike patches, and acutely venomous spines. Clothed in this deceptive patchwork, scorpionfishes sit motionless on the sea floor, waiting for fish which haven't noticed them to swim nearby, and when this happens, they open their large mouths and lunge forward. The draw created as the mouth opens is sufficient in some cases to pull in the victim.

Scorpionfishes are not the only camouflaged hazard awaiting reef fishes. The longlure frogfish and peacock flounder, with their blotchy skin patterns, are equally difficult to spot. For a better view of the fishes swimming above, the eyes of the peacock flounder are located on stalks at the top of its flat head.

The reef's countless holes, tunnels, and galleries, filled with inhabitants of all sizes, harbor some jack-in-the-box hunters like moray eels, whose long bodies suddenly erupt from nowhere as they seize their prey. The sinuous length and fierce-looking teeth of these eels seem particularly alarming to humans with our long history of fearing and shunning snakelike animals. Like snakes, however, these beautifully patterned creatures would rather avoid us than attack.

On the reef, where so many species thrive and compete, predators specialize in exploiting clearly defined depths and reef terrain. Just as stonefish keep to the bottom and eels to the reef's interior, smaller hunters like the hawkfishes frequent the branching upper areas of corals. From these treelike vantage points, hawkfishes look down at the smaller reef creatures below and lance out from time to time like an owl or a hawk, making deadly, perfectly timed swoops.

Some hunters use no camouflage, but patrol in the open, relying on brute power and speed, the traits we usually associate with larger predators. On the reef, jacks and barracudas will often swim close to potential prey, plainly in view but temporarily uninterested. However, once appetite or a choice opportunity triggers interest, they move with astonishing swiftness to consume their victims.

The sea's most notorious hunters are the sharks, and in the natural marine order, they are apex predators—nothing preys on them. An order of creatures as old as corals or crinoids, sharks include among their 300 species inshore dwellers like the gray reef shark of the Pacific and the Caribbean reef shark, often found near the reef, and ocean-going or pelagic species which rarely visit the reef. Their hunting ability is sharpened by an unusual sensitivity to the electromagnetic fields given off by other creatures, a kind of natural radar that supplements their sight, hearing, and sense of smell.

Despite their reputed ferocity, most sharks are extremely wary around humans. And with good reason. While we fire our imaginations with stories of bathers being eaten alive, sport and commercial fishermen are rapidly reducing shark populations. These fascinating creatures, which play a vital role in marine ecosystems and which have never posed much of a threat to humanity, now face as great a threat from us as anything they've encountered in millions of years.

RED HERMIT
CRAB, *Paguristes
cadenati*,
BONAIRE.
*Wearing a
mollusk's
abandoned
shell, the red
hermit crab
scavenges for
scraps from the
meals of other
predators.*

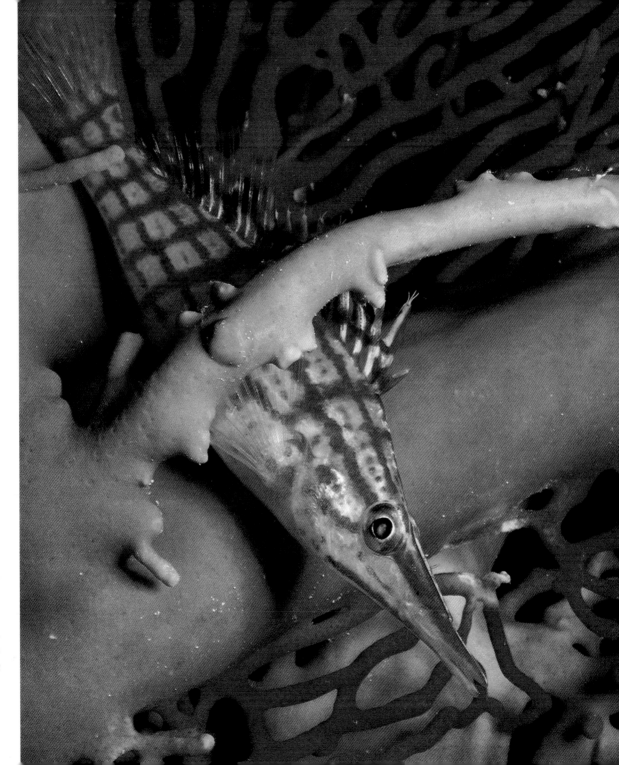

LIZARDFISH, *Synodus variegatus*, AND FALSE CLEANER BLENNY, *Aspidontus taeniatus*, NAMENALALA BARRIER REEF. *Lizardfishes lie motionless on a reef surface, then shoot out to seize their prey.*

LONGNOSE HAWKFISH, *Oxycirrhites typus*, BENGGA LAGOON, FIJI. *The hawkfish's pronounced eye sockets indicate sophisticated eye muscles and a degree of binocular vision.*

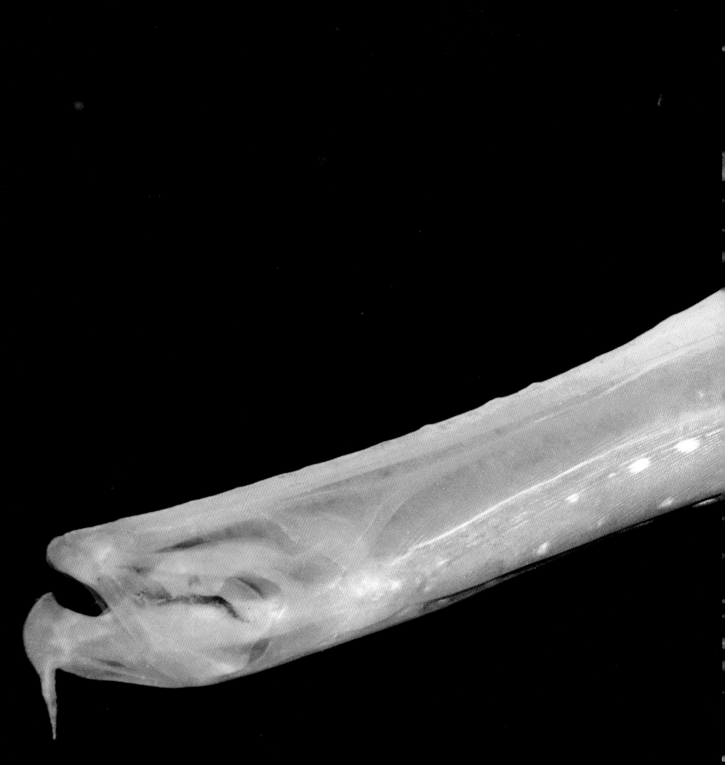

TRUMPETFISH,
*Aulustomus
maculatus*,
BONAIRE.
*Approaching its
prey nose first,
the pencil-shaped,
two-foot-long
trumpetfish
appears
deceptively small.*

ARC-EYED
HAWKFISH,
*Paracirrhites
arcuatus,* NORTH
ASTROLABE REEF.
*To perch
motionless for
long periods,
hawkfishes rely
on their thicker-
than-average
pectoral fins,
which spread out
below the gills,
propping the
fish firmly in
a crevice.*

HAWKSBILL TURTLE, *Eretmochelys imbricata*, TRIGGER ROCK, FIJI. *One of the reef's few reptiles, the hawksbill turtle feeds on sponges and jellyfish. Harvested for its translucent shell, the hawksbill is now threatened.*

SPOTFIN LIONFISH, *Pterois antennata*, NORTH ASTROLABE REEF. *The lionfish often hunts in the half-light of dawn and dusk, when its fluttering pectoral fins blend in with soft corals and crinoids.*

GOLDENTAIL
MORAY EEL,
*Gymnothorax
miliaris*, BONAIRE.
*The elusive
goldentail grows
to a length of
about a foot and
can be found in
crevices on
Caribbean reefs.*

RED-SPOTTED
HAWKFISH,
*Amblycirrhites
pinos*, BONAIRE.
*The Caribbean's
only hawkfish
species is often
found amid the
rocks and corals
of the reef
bottom.*

Symbiosis

CORAL TROUT,
Cephalopholis
miniatus, AND
CLEANER SHRIMP,
Periclimenes sp.,
NAMENALALA
BARRIER REEF.

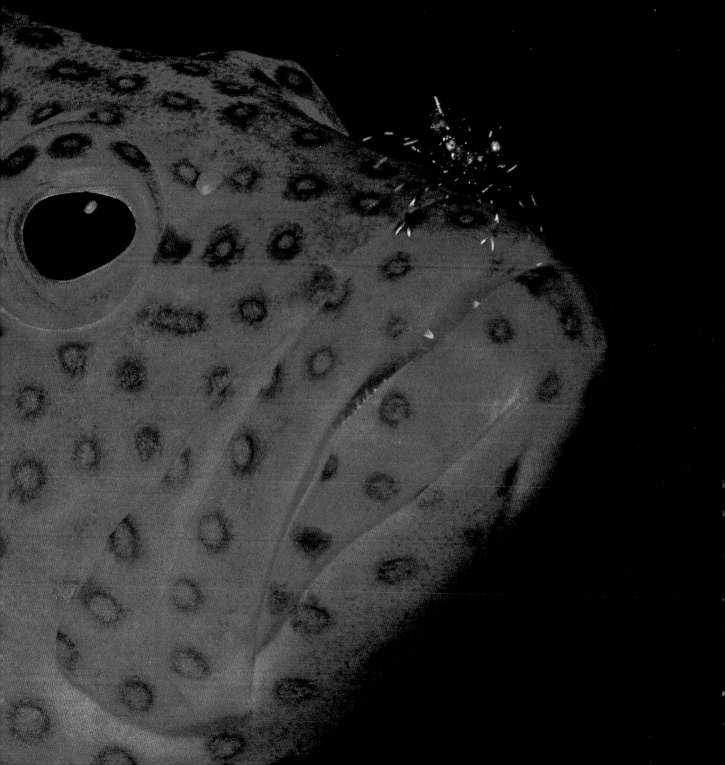

When a bristleworm crawls up a gorgonian coral like a hornworm caterpillar on a thriving tomato plant, stripping every limb clean, the relationship is predatorial, winner take all. The bristleworm gets all the polyps, and the gorgonian dies.

When a pilotfish swims within the bow-wave of a shark's snout, both are predators. But a second relationship is also operating. Potentially prey, the pilotfish has deftly positioned itself where neither sharks nor other predators can reach it. From there, it can seek smaller targets or feed on scraps from the shark's meals.

The entire life of the reef is built upon arrangements like these, in which one creature derives benefits from another; they are as vital to the reef's success as all the predatorial relationships we've described. Like a city whose prosperity continually draws new settlers, the reef is a prime place of opportunity in the sea, a place where success as an ecological organization is the engine for further specialization and differentiation.

There are many degrees of cooperation between species. In the center of the spectrum, commensal relationships—one creature feeding in the shelter of another—form a broad category with many variations. The sheltered creature benefits, and the sheltering one is at least relatively unharmed by the other's presence. An anemonefish living within a sea anemone's stinging tentacles appears to do nothing for its host, but owes its survival to those tentacles, which keep predators away. Some researchers indicate that the anemonefish takes the relationship a step further. Not only is the anemone its home and the base from which it snatches at plankton, but the mucous layer and necrotic tissue on the anemone's surface are another source of food, one which the anemone provides at little cost to its health.

In parasitic relationships, the guest dines exclusively on the substance of its host. However, unlike a true predator, which promptly ends the life of its prey, the parasite takes only as much as the host can afford to lose. When an isopod attaches itself to the flesh of a grouper, the grouper becomes less healthy, but not dangerously so.

At the other extreme are a multitude of mutualistic relationships, where both species clearly benefit. No relationship illustrates the idea better than the one on which the entire reef system is founded, the interaction between corals and zooxanthellae described in the first chapter. So efficient is the exchange of nutrients that corals are estimated to derive only 20 percent of their sustenance from the plankton and detritus they take in through their tentacles. Furthermore, zooxanthellae are clearly essential to the secretion of the calcium carbonate of which the reef is made.

Debate continues about how algae speed up the rate at which corals secrete their calcareous dwellings. One theory holds that phosphates can inhibit the crystallization of the minerals which become calcium carbonate. As algae consume those phosphates, keeping the coral polyp clean, the polyp's mineral secretions may crystallize much faster.

This is symbiosis on a submicroscopic level, and divers only see the results. A symbiotic relationship which divers can witness is that of the cleaner shrimps, wrasses, and gobies, which make themselves available to fishes which need to have parasites—mostly tiny crustaceans such as copepods and isopods—picked off their eyes, mouths, and gills. Equipped with pincerlike teeth or claws, the cleaners gently yank out these creatures, a process many observers believe the fish enjoys.

To make themselves available, the cleaning species have two tactics: they routinely position themselves in the same area, and they share certain visual cues which biologists call "guild signs." Thus the cleaning wrasses of the Pacific and the cleaning gobies of the Caribbean all have bright stripes on their sides—evidence, some say, that cleaners existed long before the tropical oceans were separated. The cleaning shrimp, too, are clearly marked with long white antennae. While gobies stake out a coral head or other landmark as their cleaning station, individual cleaning shrimp wait in a confined space, or in an anemone's tentacles, depending on the species.

For the cleaning species, the parasites are sustenance. The cleaned fishes also benefit, as we do when we pull off leeches or ticks. Cleaning must be important; despite the fact that cleaner fishes and shrimps are tasty morsels whose role causes them to swim in and around the mouths of voracious predators, they are rarely eaten by their clients. However, Greg Brown reports that he once saw a grouper shut its mouth on a cleaning shrimp "kind of absentmindedly—as if the grouper had forgotten the little shrimp was a cleaner, not a meal."

WHITE-STRIPED ANEMONEFISH, *Amphiprion perideraion*, GREAT WHITE WALL. *These anemonefish remain juveniles for long periods, living with a mated pair of adults. When one of the adults dies, the dominant juvenile matures, becoming whatever sex is needed in the mating pair.*

DOUBLE-BAR ANEMONEFISH, *Amphiprion chrysopterus*, RAINBOW REEF, FIJI. *Habituated to the anemone's stings, double-bar anemonefish spend their nights amid their host's tentacles and their days hovering nearby.*

SAWCHEEK
CARDINALFISH,
*Apogon
quadrisquamatus*,
BONAIRE.
*The reclusive but
widespread
sawcheek is the
only cardinalfish
which lives among
the stinging
tentacles of
the giant sea
anemone.*

GRAYSBY, *Cephalopholis cruentatus,* PEDERSON'S CLEANER SHRIMP, *Periclimenes pedersoni,* AND CLEANING GOBY, *Gobiosoma genie,* BONAIRE. *Often on Caribbean reefs, gobies and Pederson's cleaner shrimp share cleaning duties.*

ANEMONE SHRIMP, *Periclimenes yucatanicus,* BONAIRE. *These ornate crustaceans frequent the tentacles of the giant anemone, where they eat dead tissue.*

FLOWERY ROCK COD, *Epinephelus fuscoguttatus*, DUFF REEF, FIJI. *This cleaning wrasse works mostly around the flowery rock cod's eyes, mouth, and gills, where the largest number of parasites attach themselves.*

GOLDEN DAMSELFISH, *Amblyglyphidodon aureus*, AND CLEANING WRASSE, *Labroides dimidiatus*, NGEMELIS WALL, PALAU. *The golden damselfish extends its dorsal and pectoral fins for cleaning.*

Survival
Strategies

SEAFAN GOBY,
Bryaninops sp.,
NAMENALALA
BARRIER REEF.

In a sense, everything that every species does on the reef is a survival strategy. Even sleeping fishes take precautions — mostly by hiding, but sometimes in more specific ways. Certain species of sleeping parrotfishes envelop themselves in a mucous bubble. It's believed that this contains any smells they might give off, and may also taste unpleasant. A triggerfish, once it is parked in a reef niche, can lock its dorsal fins in place against the walls, making it impossible for a predator to haul it out.

Looking at specific ways in which reef dwellers protect themselves, we discover that some methods are used in one form or another by large numbers of species, while others are unique adaptations. As in other parts of the natural world, camouflage is a preeminent tactic.

The strobe flash of the camera sometimes gives us a distorted sense of the reef's color scheme. Below 30 feet or so, everything is partially obscured in the water's deep blue; the brilliant reds and yellows of photographs are actually unobtrusive shades of brown and taupe. At 60 feet, the loud purple bodies and yellow trim of certain flatworms look merely black as they crawl across

a seahorse hanging onto the base of a soft coral is equally inconspicuous. the bottom, and the golden yellow of

Many sea creatures not only start out with colors and patterns that blend into their surroundings, they also change them at will to suit the circumstances. Greg Brown recalls several dives when a trumpetfish, which often conceals itself by hanging in the water next to gorgonian branches or other long objects, aligned itself vertically along his strobe's support arm. As the fish hung there, it slowly changed its skin color to the blue of the strobe arm. For a moment, Greg was an accomplice to the trumpetfish's predatory plans.

These kinds of color changes are made possible by a complex arrangement of cells that carry melanin, guanine, and carotenoids. A large number of fishes can make rapid changes in the brightness of their skin by regulating the amount of melanin in certain cells. It's not unusual, for example, to see a bright red grouper at a cleaning station blanch temporarily — perhaps making its parasites easier to see.

Many fishes, particularly motionless camouflage artists like the scorpionfishes, also adjust carotene levels over longer periods to adapt to the color scheme of their hiding spot. Some members of the family go further, encouraging algal growth on their skin.

Crustaceans are less adept at changing color, but have compensated in other ways. Some hermit crabs, the so-called decorator crabs, stick patches of algae and sponge atop the borrowed shells in which they live. One species places sea anemones on top of its shell: the anemone's food supply is increased by the hermit crab's movements, and the crab gains additional protection as a result of the anemone's presence. One type of anemone even seeks out these hermit crabs, jumping onto a passing crab's shell.

While some reef creatures do their best to hide, others seem determined to stand out. Closer to the surface, the sun brings out color, and here the brilliant patterns of damselfishes, angelfishes, and butterflyfishes cry out for attention. The laws of survival are strict enough that there should be a solid reason for these fishes' visibility. But while many theories have been proposed, none is universally accepted.

Fishes are also conspicuous when they school, and many species do at different times. However, a school of *Anthias* swimming near a grouper is protected in the same way as a herd of gazelles grazing near a lioness. To make a kill, the hunter needs a clear target, and with so many creatures so close together, it's difficult to make a choice until a straggler breaks ranks.

In one way, schooling fishes differ remarkably from herding animals. The coordination of their movements, even in huge aggregations, is flawless: the school turns together without any fish missing the mysterious cue.

The perfect coordination which divers marvel at in schooling fishes might be taken as a symbol for the coordination of life throughout the reef. Here is a world encompassing thousands of different species, bound together by millions of bonds of cooperation or competition. As we begin to consider attaining a less wasteful and destructive way of life for ourselves, this underwater world, where nothing is wasted, can be read as an example of all that is right with nature. We may never achieve, or even want, societies as highly organized as the reef ecosystem. But let us hope that we become organized enough—and civilized enough—to preserve the reefs we have from our reckless experiment in global consumerism.

BARRACUDAS, *Sphyraena sp.*, NAVATU ATOLL, FIJI. *Even barracudas, feared predators of many reef species, school for protection when sharks or dogtooth tuna are near.*

LONGFIN BANNERFISH, *Heniochus acuminatus*, WAKAYA PASSAGE, FIJI. *Like many butterflyfishes, longfin bannerfish appear to pair for life, an adaptation which may help this territorial species defend its home.*

GLASSFISH, *Parapriacanthus guentheri*, STINGRAY STATION, RED SEA. *Schooling fishes like these glassfish often have a wide field of vision, enabling them to respond instantly to a predator's movements.*

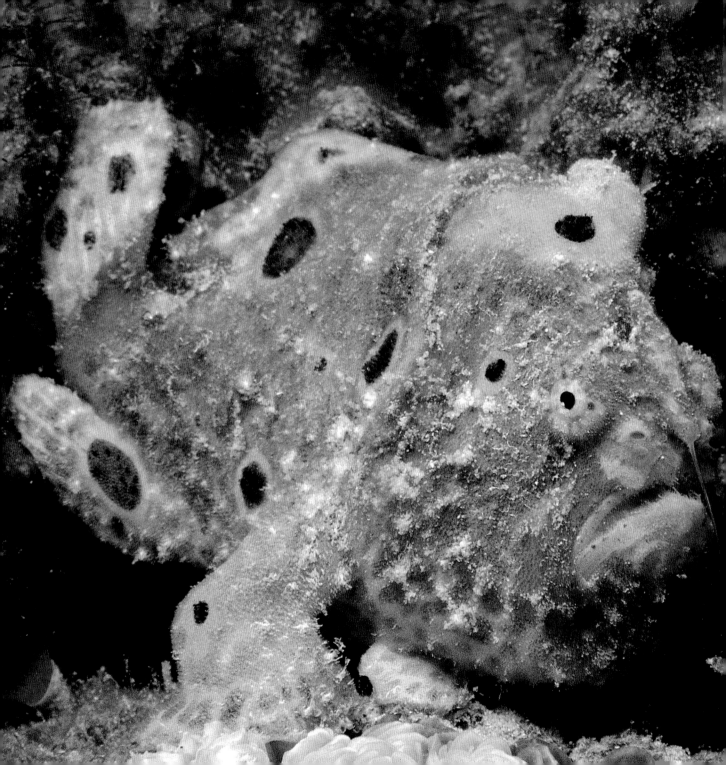

LONGLURE
FROGFISH,
*Antennarius
multiocellatus*,
BONAIRE.
*Sitting perfectly
still on the reef
bottom, the
frogfish wiggles
a lure on its
forehead to attract
other fish within
swallowing
range.*

SCORPIONFISH,
Scorpaenopsis sp.,
GREAT WHITE
WALL, FIJI.
*The lethargic
scorpionfish's
encrusted skin
renders it
virtually invisible
to prey, and its
venomous spines
discourage
predators.*

PURPLE-BLOTCHED
BASSLETS, *Anthias
pleurotania*,
GREAT WHITE
WALL, FIJI.
(BACKGROUND)
*The purple-
blotched basslet,
like other* Anthias
*species, can
change its sex
and looks.*
(INSET) *Yellow
basslets are
young females
swimming in
groups under a
dominant male.
When males die,
leading females
replace them,
assuming their
purple coloring.*

ORANGE-BALL
ANEMONE,
*Pseudocorynactis
caribboreum,*
BONAIRE.
*Only when
feeding at night
do the tentacles
of the sparsely
distributed orange-
ball anemone
protrude from its
concealed base.*

(INSET)
SHARPNOSE
PUFFERFISH,
*Canthigaster
rostratum,*
BONAIRE.
*This two-inch-
long puffer
is a secretive,
omnivorous
grazer. At night
it rests by
hugging close
to corals and
sponges for
protection.*

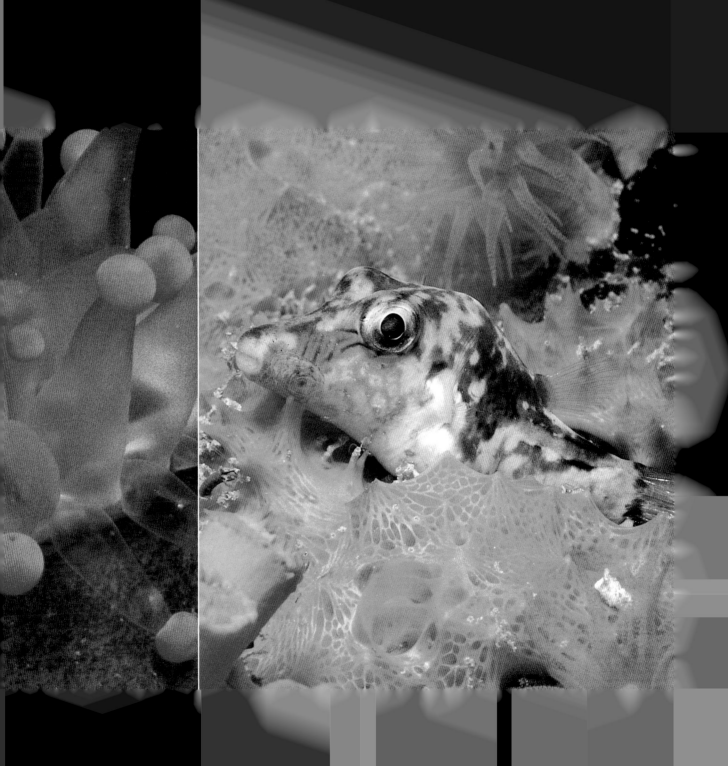

BLUE TANG,
*Acanthurus
coeruleus,*
BONAIRE.
*At night the
blue tang attempts
to remain incon-
spicuous among
the sponges and
corals of the
Caribbean.*

BRITTLE STAR,
*Ophiothrix
purpurea,* PALAU.
*The brittle star
can move quickly
when disturbed. If
a pursuer grabs a
limb, the limb
breaks off,
allowing the
brittle star
to escape.*

Taking pictures underwater can be an exhilarating experience. It can also be a frustrating, nightmarish event. Because I've been on both sides of the fence, I hope to pass along some suggestions that might help your underwater photographic efforts.

I was just a plain old scuba diver long before I became an obsessed underwater photographer. Those early diving days turned out to be very important—before I heard of a Nikonos, I was relaxed underwater and possessed good diving skills. With few exceptions, this is the first step to success.

Once your diving skills are adequately tuned, the next objective is to select a camera system capable of producing the kinds of photos you wish to take. No one lens or camera can do it all; research your needs carefully, and select the right equipment for the task. The images in this book were taken with a variety of cameras, lenses, strobes, and films. The small- to medium-sized reef organisms were photographed using a Nikon F3 with a DA-2 actionfinder in a housing. The lenses employed were 55mm and 105mm Micro-Nikkors. For the wide-angle scenes, I used a Nikonos camera with either a 15mm or 28mm lens. The primary strobe for both macro and wide-angle work was the Ikelite Substrobe 225. A second, slave strobe (Sonic Research 2000) was used for some scenes. I used the Kodachrome series films and Fujichrome's Velvia.

Photographing subjects under water is, in most instances, another form of wildlife photography. Successful wildlife photographers know their subjects intimately. Many animals, especially marine organisms, are more easily approached during specific times of day. Understanding subtle nuances is helpful in creating a worthy image.

Another trait ingrained in top wildlife photographers is perhaps the single most important aspect of successful underwater photography: infinite patience. In the world below, frustration levels can build rapidly. Strobes fail to flash, sync cords won't sync, cameras leak, visibility stinks, and the prettiest fish move near the speed of light. Mantas and whale sharks always show up when you're outfitted with a lens that won't work on them.

Underwater photography is a game of inches. The closer you can get to your subject, the less water you shoot through. Less water means fewer silt particles, better image detail, and more color saturation. When it seems close enough, it's not. Move closer. Closer. Now take the picture.

In an environment where many organisms are adapted to blend with their surroundings, contrast is an important concept, which is why upward camera angles generally work well. When tilting the lens up, you give the subject greater contrast by framing it against a blue water background.

Even with the right temperament, the right tools, and the proper knowledge, there is still a large margin for error. That's why the pros bracket. Bracketing means taking the picture at the believed-to-be-correct f-stop, then taking a photograph of the same subject using one f-stop over and under the "correct" exposure. My version of bracketing not only entails using multiple f-stops, but also includes varying lighting and camera angles and switching strobe power settings. Don't hesitate to expose numerous frames of a cooperative subject. Chances are you've traveled too far to risk taking only one or two pictures.

If your camera system goes underwater only once or twice a year, then your photographs will probably look like those taken by a vacationing diver. Practice mastering your system year round in a pool or a lake. Don't expect to dust off the equipment twice a year, take it to paradise for a week, and churn out quality images.

Indeed, diving in paradise invariably poses yet another pitfall to underwater photographers—that compulsive need to have a picture of everything with gills. Ask yourself this: do you want a thousand mediocre pictures or 20 to 30 great ones? If you suspect a scene has little chance of being a reasonably good picture, don't waste the film. If it didn't look too good through the viewfinder, it won't look that good on the exposed film.

I've spoken these words to diving photographers all over the world. Maybe some of it strikes home, but more than likely your skills will be developed by getting wet, exposing lots of film, and making mistakes. That's how I learned.

Enjoy your time in the sea taking photographs, and share your images with others as often as possible. To record on film what the mind envisions is, after all, to preserve for everyone a glimpse of your fondest memories.
—W. Gregory Brown

Few people are more appreciative of the splendor of coral than divers. Ironically, through inadvertent contact with the reef, these same divers account for untold damage to the environments they treasure. This is an area where individual behavior can and does have a direct ecological impact. By learning to be aware of the effects of all underwater actions, divers can minimize accidental reef damage. In doing so, they can also discover a new way of appreciating marine life and habitats, one based more on observation than on interaction.

1. DETERMINE WHICH PORTIONS OF THE REEF CAN BE TOUCHED WITHOUT DOING HARM. Whether you are wearing gloves or not, you should always move slowly and touch only what you know your contact will not damage—sand patches, granite substrate, coral rubble. Before you use your hands, use your eyes, and remember that even the "dead" parts of the reef are habitats for living creatures. Never kneel on the reef. Once it becomes second nature to plan all contacts with the reef, divers can readily steady or pull themselves along the bottom with a carefully placed fingertip if unexpected strong currents make this necessary.

Photographers should brace themselves in appropriate areas to get the shots they want—relying on neutral buoyancy can lead to inadvertent damage as the photographer, preoccupied with making an image, settles on the reef or stirs sand with his flippers. For this reason, you should use mounted rather than handheld strobes. If you cannot take a particular shot without inflicting damage to the reef, move on to something else. Those who take more than one camera system underwater on a given dive should never lay their extra equipment on vulnerable areas of the reef.

2. STREAMLINE EQUIPMENT. Take only what is essential, and secure that equipment close to the body. Excess straps and webbing should be eliminated where feasible. Ideally, nothing should hang below the diver. Keep in mind that slipping is inevitable; check the position of your gauges throughout your dive.

3. KICK WITH CARE. Sand stirred from the bottom can be just as destructive to the reef as a direct fin blow. To reduce accidental fin contact, select the smallest fins you can comfortably use and still swim nonstop at a moderate pace for ten to fifteen minutes without leg fatigue.

Never use a full scissors kick near the reef. A bent-knee kick, generated from the lower leg instead of the knee, is much less destructive and every bit as effective. The cave-diver's kick, generated from the calves and fin blades with legs extended and knees bent perpendicular to the body, is also useful. An ankle kick, using only the ankles and fins in a rotating or up-and-down motion won't give you power or speed, but it will give you all the control you need while working close to the coral. Don't keep kicking if your fins accidentally knock into something—relax your legs and turn to assess the situation. Gently pushing your hand against a safe area, adding air in your BCD, or sculling with your hands can help you gain the necessary clearance to kick without harm to the reef.

Buoyancy control, not kicking, is the way to approach and leave the reef. Always bend your knees and leave your fin tips pointed up as you near the coral. On leaving the area, refrain from kicking until your fins are clear of the bottom.

Photographers especially should refrain from kicking to minimize the possibility of stirring up silt—it looks terrible in photographs.

4. DEVELOP BUOYANCY CONTROL SKILLS. Most divers carry more weight than they need. If at the end of a dive when your tank is nearly empty, you cannot maintain neutral buoyancy at ten feet without pumping air into your BCD, you are overweight. Always adjust your weight belt to your current level of expertise and wear it in the waist position that allows you to swim horizontally with your feet elevated. Alter its position throughout your dive as necessary. Your tank's position in the backpack can also be manipulated to help you maintain correct balance. Fine-tune your buoyancy through breath control, and remember that greater depths require greater attentiveness—don't be so overwhelmed by the wonders you may see

there that you forget this basic diving tenet and fail to compensate for the natural loss of buoyancy through wetsuit compression in deep water.

Photographers should bear in mind that carrying a camera both changes their balance and affects their buoyancy.

5. KEEP INTERACTION WITH MARINE LIFE TO A MINIMUM. Respect wildlife for what it is—wild. Always seek the advice of local experts before handling any creature; if you don't know how to interact with the wildlife without harming it, leave it alone. Study the individual's reaction to you. A seemingly innocent ride on a sea turtle can leave it exhausted and vulnerable to predation. Regardless of their behavior, these animals are not tame. As fun as it may seem, riding or feeding wildlife is never a good idea.

Photographers should resist the temptation to manipulate marine life to get a desired image—such a photograph is unlikely to be an improvement on what nature has already provided.

6. ANCHOR RESPONSIBLY. All heavily dived areas should be equipped with moorings. If there are none, boats can safely be tied to the reef using the same criteria for any reef contact. Smaller craft can also be hand anchored. Thoughtlessly placed anchors and anchor chains devastate coral; dive-tour operators who toss anchors blindly onto a reef should be boycotted.

P H O T O G R A P H S